"A key imperative in Marjorie Welish's superb new book, *A Complex Sentence*, is the task of 'not writing the unsaid,' which presumably would mean to write the sayable in the folds of a complex sentence that erases it. Literary spirit guides come along to help—Mallarmé, Hopkins, Pound. There may be a ghostly revision of Pound's imagism, 'a complex in an instant of time,' but instead of le mot juste, we have le mot détourné, diverted as it enters into new semiotic fields and explodes. *A Complex Sentence* is, in addition, a meditation on the book—its materiality (pages, margins, indexes, parchment, epigraphs, sentences)—and its cultural role as a document. Welish's sentences *are* complex, grammatically and narratively; they break the spine, as it were, of the book's monumentality. In the interstices of writing and saying lies the supplement to meaning, what we read between the lines or what the lines—center margined or flush left—arrange as a new structure of understanding. This is a wild and compelling book."
                                                                    —Michael Davidson

"*A Complex Sentence* is an important book in more than one understanding. It is important in its gather from the range of comprehensions and tentative elusions that comprise Marjorie Welish's considerable range of work. It is important in that it stands out as seminal in a context of the large number of contemporary poetry book publications. This has come about from the joyful complexity of an artist with visual acuity and constructivist practice in tow with an exact sense of word choice and recurrence. It is a book of poetry that stands out in its range of attentions to different modes of construction and is cohesive in its interconnectivity between each construction, between stanzas between different poems between different visual presentations. There is a clarity in the book's musicality and a disruption of clarity in its sensitive juxtapositions. This is Welish at her best and most powerful moments, at moments of loss and gain, at moments of assuredness and in fleets of frailty."
                                                                        —Allen Fisher

"In 'Pervasive Spacing,' one of several key signature (as in a musical com-position and guide to binding pages) poems in *A Complex Sentence,* Marjorie Welish pauses her restless pencil (instrument of inscription and erasure) to assert this axiomatic one-liner: 'Scale: she was larger than the room in which she found herself.' So too Welish, a practitioner of conceptual writ-ing long before the phrase entered the zeitgeist of contemporary American poetry. Her procedural writing, à la Mac Low et al., exceeds normative critical and poetic categories. *A Complex Sentence* is the latest instantiation of Welish's relentless pursuit and demonstration of her deliberate, delim-ited, and far-reaching conceptual imagination. More forcefully than ever before, she subjects found and 'original' texts to a panoply of formal con-straints. Roaming across the vistas of Western writing—Cicero, Epictetus, Edmund Burke, William Strode, Ezra Pound, Bertolt Brecht, William Carlos Williams, and Nathaniel Mackey all make cameo appearances—Welish cuts and pastes texts into frames of intertextuality, disseminating critical glosses, free-floating quotations, and judgments that, though grounded in a commitment to the primacy of aesthetics, are unafraid of political, social, and cultural affirmations and rebuttals. Welish's wide-ranging metapoems excavate the generative assumptions underlying the production and trans-latability of verbal, plastic, and musical languages. *A Complex Sentence* strips bare the book, canvas, drawing board, and score, jettisoning their accumu-lated histories in order to resituate them within the domains of languages as denaturalized artifacts. Moreover, media per se is reduced to so many per-mutations of spacing, rendering temporality and, by implication, aesthetic 'readability' as effects, per Derrida, of différance. Encoding her writing as both normative spacing and non-spacing markings (diacritics being a prime example of the latter), Welish treats morphemes as both analog and digi-tal codes mapped onto materials that are anything but neutral. Displacing semantics with syntactics, foregrounding the syntagmatic over the para-digmatic, Welish reminds her readers of the structural, formal, and, above all, cultural values that constrain all meaning-making, artistic or not. For these reasons and more, the title of this book must be read simultaneously as a dialectics—adjective-noun, adjective-verb, noun-verb—without reso-lution, three dyads orbiting one another in the dance of an intellect with few peers."

—Tyrone Williams

A COMPLEX

SENTENCE

Also by Marjorie Welish

The Annotated "Here" and Selected Poems

Word Group

Isle of the Signatories

In the Futurity Lounge / Asylum for Indeterminacy

So What So That

A COMPLEX SENTENCE

Marjorie Welish

COFFEE HOUSE PRESS
Minneapolis
2021

The cover art is a page from book 3 of the *Codex Justinianus* and includes marginal glosses. Image is courtesy of the Free Library of Philadelphia, Rare Book Department.

Coffee House Press books are available to the trade through our primary distributor, Consortium Book Sales & Distribution, cbsd.com or (800) 283-3572. For personal orders, catalogs, or other information, write to info@coffeehousepress.org.

Coffee House Press is a nonprofit literary publishing house. Support from private foundations, corporate giving programs, government programs, and generous individuals helps make the publication of our books possible. We gratefully acknowledge their support in detail in the back of this book.

LIBRARY OF CONGRESS CATALOGING-IN-PUBLICATION DATA

Names: Welish, Marjorie, 1944– author.
Title: A complex sentence / Marjorie Welish.
Identifiers: LCCN 2020052679 | ISBN 9781566896085 (paperback)
Subjects: LCGFT: Poetry.
Classification: LCC PS3573.E4565 C66 2021 | DDC 811/.54—dc23
LC record available at https://lccn.loc.gov/2020052679

PRINTED IN THE UNITED STATES OF AMERICA

28 27 26 25 24 23 22 21   1 2 3 4 5 6 7 8

Contents

A COMPLEX

SENTENCE

Itself

Sedentary in another language is language as such

Whether or not we can read it, sought

Because home. Inscription composted

space works this interrogation of me:

"You have a nice listening face,"

Inspection shining forth.

You face + the animal kingdom.

There once was transparency near the face

Hexagonal in facets blown vehemently and so heated

Green purple orange near and flush

Edges with much interest in their complements at vertices—

I refer to red yellow blue should you look through

The tumbler's flaring solar sonar crystal

For the 18th-century beverage: light.

Fixtures, Gloves, Moonlight

Radiated emitted body   incandescent spot flood   arm leg wing beak
neck feathered close proximity even soft even lighted areas   mound
hoard of boxes   bunched tilt glacial   expulse shards of temper pulling
evening harmony along with it   simulated scope steadily pulling
simulation   along with in into the still central lifelessness.   View the
drape mound   date time the pulling of which reveals linoleum of the
studio pose the stand on which the still life supposing the mound of the
ear an earful of chromaticism in extra amounts mounts the sentence.

Living no note mutet	off / off
In death voiced sound	off / on
Sang first last no more	on / off
Farewell all o death come	on / on
(arguably welcome farewell	on / on)

The reproach is interesting

End

Pronounced

1

Farewell recital
Of the swan in faceless ice
Is frontal affectlessness
But for lips extruded pursuant to
A classic plosive.
A penny's worth spat out.

2

Infinity, a dead end
Unlikeable it sayeth only
A parameter wherein with lips'
Handy dispenser box
Derives horror.

Frontal swan
Whose drop-down menu fundamental
Shovels a silver breeze
You for me in yours.

Frozen for me in your
Cinema of long takes.

3

To pose

simulacra

Your beak's skill set

With it: a still life and that past

Scenographic *Parsifal*

Swan never: that

Opening shot.

Whose

Lip-synched

Wires are these

Emitting from the impossibly long

Neck of series.

In Recital

Not
Eyes ears
Facial

Lips pronounced
Other not eyes ears
Nose thought

Deleted
Noncompliant
Eyes ears

To see the eliminated
Very eyes fixed an odyssey collect
All ears nose throat

These not
Vaster vellum
Of resident lips

Facially noncompliant
To not see is to hear to smell to
Express lips all the more

Recital.
Lips nonchalant underserved
Testy specificity of.

Skywatching

1

The activity of attending films at the cinema   . . . *of going to see motion*
pictures   . . . *of going to see motion pictures*   incessant habit of moviegoing

to serve   wait upon   to put in play severe   stringent
futurity   apart arguably icy

tomorrow. In preterition
auld lang syne   ages ago   old long since   times past yesterday

Today to serve   wait upon to put in play
auld lang syne's habitual moviegoing

Yesterday today tomorrow   icy   moviegoing

2

The activity of attending films at the cinema
Severe
Auld lang syne

The act of going regularly to watch films at the cinema
Many severally
this in the manner of our ancestors

. . . *of going to see motion pictures*
to serve wait upon
preterition

frequenting the movies
a pilot
in times past

The activity of attending films at the cinema
Severe aura in the well-wrought
Auld lang syne

The act of going regularly to watch films at the cinema
Severally morning noon and binoculars
this in the manner of our ancestors

Glacial moons through staring
to serve wait upon
. . . *of going to see motion pictures*

At noon today   preterition
frequenting the movies
apart   arguably icy

fatigue
as when *past is prologue*
yesterday today tomorrow

aircraft aspirational but
with astringent
time.

The activity of attending films at the cinema
Yesterday's long exposure
turns its back on

tomorrow. Apart arguably icy
auld lang syne's incessant
habitual moviegoing

how the spot
segmental yesterday today
tomorrow's glacial kiss has sped up

the very polemic. Filmic
long ago since
severs severally into movement

although not so equidistant:
yesterday today tomorrow   icy   moviegoing
Yesterday Today Tomorrow, icy   moviegoing

3

The door is opening.
The doors open at noon.

Raising a Storm

*[T]he paths he had marked for himself, but who had a
tendency to allow esoteric lore to become an unduly
important part of his poetry. This tendency continues . . .*

From *Oxford Companion to American Literature*

Would it be just to return weapons to a madman?

in his translation of . . .

Raising a storm   the furor that rages up the Archimedean spout: ink
battlespirit   slaughter on Tenth Avenue   homeopathic funeral games
to defend against   the dull   bureaucrat   sent to cut. Dispatched to cut
you he says "give me the title" or "give me the name" or "give me your
friend—no, just the gown"   to abrogate dark matter without the quarrel,
and unable to restrain himself, no longer immune.

He swore you are that time's sorrow

Seeing red and raising a storm through the spout   ink to battle mediocre
bureaucrat sent to cut stalks to divert social network to divest your name
of obscure pains' formidable spear arcane to someone in the terrible
foreshadowing: and what is metallurgy? Seeing red furor to fermented
epilogue of consequence to others   a firestorm of paper   unable to
restrain itself   no longer arcane, engulfing that which he writes: Let the
Greater Not Pass Me. Let the Obscure Be Cold and same gambit or Let
the Lost Be Worthless   obscured cold platform. Had again.   To cut you
the bureaucrat exacts: I Promise You subject verb object, subject verb
object, at last!

Quiver: blazon

He began to scatter his interests

To say that this chromata-retaliating barb is nothing is to spurn
chromata-retaliatory razor wire from whence cometh my help

*and became a leader of the . . . [. . .] and sponsored diverse authors
and wrote much*

and so return pox, spousal strife, feuds never-ending, and starvation.

*about his successive enthusiasms, later generally acknowledged as
significant.*

Then, I defy you stars. Then I deny you, stars. Staves, true or false?

Heat raising a storm of magnets'   seeing red ink from cut   stalks
his conscience or sprouts a choke hold on abductors. From your tear
ducts, a tidal tremble informed the funeral games throughout the later
Cantos

And who is he who would of you savor saying that, would say that
incompetent dart.

Let the Weapons Yield to Humanities   Bespoke you had Jefferson
write   turning up the fire putting the heat on magnets   unintimidated
ambergris   I quench a glance in your direction, seized. Splinters *About
You* as obscure thereby lost   in thought seeing red raising a storm
turning the heat up incommensurable fitness—give me your terminology,
the guy said   that guy who does not know.

Homeless funeral games contrary in you about whom it will have been
said he had a talent for setting fire to his lives. Raising a storm: Are your
curricula rigorous? And do your graduates lead meaningful lives? From
cut stalks, you, the heat on magnets and ambergris as a preservative.
Long ago, make your mark! Let the record show   gauntlet so tired that
speaking hurts. Let the weapons yield to plan   elevation   still stinging
you aspired to   plan

              became leader of the Imagists

became the terror's exacting the sediment of the demand   lore
louver   obscurity to divert divest star demand detonate detour key
clarity not where you are: obscuring sharp knife quill loaves fishes
lore such black wove stuff the eye traveling   downward and between
which less   more knowingly   is the gray diction to and from force's
softer brush with you, diadem. Between which is the softer diesel
detaining you.

Quiver: the art

              Those he championed included . . .

              A talent for promise.
              A talent argent.
              Oh, that.
Require also a talent for camouflage   as shiny reflection to break
up silhouette in sky attain to illegibility for safe passage   in combat
impressions   I shall now do my rendition of wit   to vomit scintillation
A scattering extempore *did more to win the War than many* of those
military decorated with trinkets

I promise stars' glassy wow splintering spirit in lag time!

[. . .] containing the first three cantos of a lengthy work, with a
flexible conversational style-like structure. His later poetry was
almost entirely devoted to these cantos . . . They are so filled with
esoteric lore and recondite theories that

Then I forswear that companion to Americana toga to be reckoned with
pith.

[. . .] yet they have had a tremendous influence on modern poetry

You had a talent for being a person of interest. Raising pots and
pans against redaction begat the song needing no passport. Raising
a storm turning to tune a rave had impact   begat songs the lore beat
for literature. Insist on letters insist that these do not obscure epic as
meanwhile epigones hide and seek hurricane deterrent   empurpled.
Skid did leave basketry did lean on Italy to have been done before
the economic miracle. We shall confer. To cut the poet, the nonentity
applied genteel heat

Absolute now must be unseated!

In a speech of epithets I would be heard: functioning on such a high
level masks your deficits   nerve surviving   the gift right there   laser
lifting dedicatory inscriptions from you, the true poet: "Although I did
not know him, his death offends my sense of justice."

Absolute now must be perforated.

Quiver: expat

Soil

Of his gift for realizing potentialities recognized in stranger unforeseen
AND OR AND NOT (grazing animals not sheep)
So I say to you

Thieves' cant wreck
Clear glass square leaning
[. . .] from whence cometh my help. My help.

Loins heart head hands neck back leg foot
I wonder as I wander
Reductive, not Minimal, strictly speaking

Parsimony *under erasure.*
In stating and restating loins in bunches
that cultivated green

chimes and harp or xylophone and pursed lips
subpoenas issued
motifs of and through sociability expressed in
        bourgeois households

Oxen-Eyed

And the question   designed to hit a distant target
Facts   drawing in liquid   forcing into a fine spray
Rhetoric   resounds when struck (with a soft mallet)
Upper-left corner   canted in disinterested beauty
Pamphlet   having a low-cut neckline   to complete or interrupt a circuit
Index   a whisk for beating chocolate into a foam
Manuscript   extending far down   extending upward from the horizon
Signature   probate inventories
Transcript   saw-toothed   to employ stratagems
Sentence   like an umbrella   able to retard a falling body

Page   to pull out   expel   to throw down in a mess
Endnotes   a study in contrasts   a restless sleep
Signature   was said to belong to   a flexible stick
Abstract   the dull terra-cotta   of marriage
Word   to make a living in the same language
Concept   to cause (or give out) several short, sharp sounds
Outline   consisting of a hard shell   to make slow
Theory   being able to travel long distances without refueling

Pencil in Pause

As in **thieves' cant wreck those engulfed**   as in perilous night with language doubling languages and

Pencil only   canted foam rests leather-weighted writing and reading meant to interview rare book for changing technologies   *implements cover the waterfront   transparent to the* area of interest, *not omitting anything of the* **calendar page that revives the verdict pursuant to aria** *to deal with all parts of a subject or area of interest   and most anything* taking a passageway through the split screen   to illuminated microphone off on   lectern spliced with a narrative that "picks up on" the sentence being deleted. Without identifying   the subject   **keys pursuant to area of interest pursuant to an arena shout "it is Greek, [therefore] it cannot be read"   logo   it is Greek roaring technologies   logo, it is Greek roaring prosthesis**   Why is he transposed? An   omnivorous reading for ulcerated printed "e." Shift key in   perforations of the writing studio   habits and prosthesis being (a desk?) on a quest for the threshold   threshold at analogue and digital technologies   *IDL (interface definition language) is a generic term for a language that lets a program or object written in one language communicate with another program written in an unknown language. In distributed object technology, it's important that new objects be able to be sent to any platform environment and discover how to run in that environment* **what is   a search table that surrounds me . . .** Zummer on prosthesis (why is he so fascinated with this?) a year spent gestating table tablet Pens pens pens! the cabinet maker's office springing from a desk the work station as it was   then   table tablet catalogue for the gaming table's magic mechanic disappearing act portable traveling writing desk for the campaign and such writing equipment as drains our imagination   a case for pens et cetera ink stick secretary's disappearing cabinetry invaginated as is Hamlet   cabinet case writing casket Caxton's advert   IF IT PLEASE ANY PIECES   PERFECT LETTER WHICH   PIECES, Pens and ink! Between these   and a year spent gesticulating.

The word   Hopkins's hairline fractures of   marking paper paper trail on paper put to paper and rendered studio circle of school of   the phrase meant a commitment to these   dare words in study. To search for the

table desk workstation designed for digital   tower monitor and keyboard
fathom no ink blotter resting on the canted stand   fathom no fountain
no wells no springs' despondent pens for writing on the   demise of the
gift the   guileless cascades   he in reckless askesis.

*Avail yourself of this and that salt   having taken steps   button prevailed
upon* analogue to read the idiom of digital poetics or of chalk marker
with red ink swearing I heard myself say swivel   to the page thank you
for reaching Caxton his urgent shout-out   or recent call meant salutary
say-so   in Aramaic trade language hello to mend that initial   signature
print name date. A year later upon waking I heard myself say: **what I
really need is a table that surrounds me . . .** aleatory to *broken logic, says
Bök: Repent pathetic script upon waking* whereupon the person . . . waking
and walking out past the storefront windows assayed many times seen
that through the open door **is a table that surrounds** and is surrounded
by items and stuff vintage recycled and such *copied distance*   what better
hunt table type styled after   school of circle of   wrought or wrought
and swivel   drop leaf implanting the bolt-latch frame extended though
adverbs   the analogy *aleatory extracting broken logic escaping through
algorithm escapade   aleatory expenditure of broken logic escaping through
Aramaic trade language.*   Act, the hunt over.

Tab tag tap **marking stones technologies of the writing studio view
habits and practices of** tap key in editorial cabinetry *pencil in shout
shout   power up pause fate face is running* to make decisions interior
through the meant door the hunt that has precise consequences but does
not cheat narrative in premature output. Know they idiom design? *An
algorithm that produces a yes or no answer is called a decision procedure; one
that leads to a solution is a computation procedure* **pencil in delay turn on if
then can do the program cannot do the program the configurations
anticipating the very action** *a lot of red ink is not always fateful*   **shout
kitchen stuff** provisions draw together a narrative upon waking touch
screen. "*This copied distance . . .*" Mallarmé Algorithm came true: **pencil
awoke parenthetical desk   don't you weep ink   found object can promise
only that there**   forfeit   a guide walking   **mesh made to eat soap**   skill
wheeling camouflage in foliage birdsong   **I promise only a locution for
utensils' uncommon valor**

A walnut is of two minds, touch and go

Indigo microtonal

Genuine leather abide with me

A word in repair   book-length words reprise healthy data

A table is not always fateful methodology of a deity

To get wind of red ink is matter to black ink

To beat the bushes with a **haughty catapult**   *a word*

extending the noise from itself   an abrasive word   a history of

mulch groove rut trench much spilt ink incrementing a counter

Staples established this as if   a feast

Implements cover the waterfront   reedy shore

The sureties shout "it is Greek, [therefore] it cannot be read"

Logo   it is Greek roaring technologies thieves' cant wreck

infinite loop for two violins, time and tide,

those engulfed copyists

That there   **skill swarms intercept** or here meant   wearing a desk
interrogative an overt signal please complete the highlighted directives
in hospital wanting to achieve a future **kit   database   at recitals   the**
turning of leaves and   touched skin pinprick   proposals to be written
make a fist flex time   don't breathe   breathe crowd to crowd a crowd
moving as group yet (assumed) mind, philosophy of   as in the staging
area for algorithmic outpatient procedures   the moving desk is differently
allocated for receiving the prick   *altering the world to match the words*
and so inciting a screen   to *a sequence of operations to be performed*   to
elicit instances for required fields prerequisites of an   author. It is Sanskrit
therefore neither drawing nor painting   insofar as a contentious line
can be read throughout as with leaf metonymy   outline drawing outline
drawing other   does become calligraphic in what kindergarten how

to   *The Natural Way to Draw* by Kimon Nicolaïdes in whose practice an
outline fixes boundary erects closure even as a *contour* fingers mass across
the topographical body   in virtue of crossing   a mass. *Look at the body
not the paper* as your charcoal feels its way across the massive rock edge
contour boundary threshold graphical representative of an intercept;
anatomically disproportionate though it may be the calligraphic quality
will be made   as matter to make to do to make a desk happen   flow from
the hunt table type   wondrous river equipped with drop leaf   a stream
from the lamp a clip-on lamp the flexible neck   of possible   dashed
lines where it is written   illuminated through an intermittent gift within
the parchment's pale metropolis   is manifest signage to that slid bolt
underneath   with difficulty with ease then to segue to   an epigram the
inscription foresaw. In pause gestating a digression   we breathe to mend
paper through adhesive   for which the restoration cannot undo what has
been done

awareness full tilt   pencil

in narrative turns on if then adhesive

realm   humid all too humid

in repairs   and tar mineral earths but we've established this   or here's
another torrent of spokenness through the interview or profile or Q
and A   itself the action of belongings: in medias res sulking in his tent;
Chekhov's rhetoric of steady state   parsimonious; metalepsis in Godard's
acknowledging Brecht's usage.

"Let a sign   stand for the words"

Selected and edited traces   chasing the categories

attired at table

contained

as are warriors

at some greater table this serves.

Some of all alarming a dying fall

Lean on their defeated shield   spear diagonally

A declension from upright indicative of being

Where doing had been   henceforth throughout   an entablature

Of itself. No other

Table   for now all we know   Posted

Struggle of lesser great categories contending

For daunting future altitude   some all no unattended other

Tableaux of desktop   with   being

Real   not a folly for foliage with sympathetic feathers   not a list

In diaspora   a palimpsest   obviously self-portraiture

Through fathers too numerous   threads

Peculiar traits found in alphabetic adjacency

some kindred   some not subroutine   a fond

instep.

Backtalk

WRITING in book   annotating

NOT-WRITING in book   writhing   sparingly

AS IS

spit

SOME

AS IS

spit out words

WRITING in book   annotating

NOT-WRITING in book   writhing   sparingly   spit

authorship

of the reader whose marginalia   we read

doubling lines   marginalia where "Dada"

impatient to be nonverbal   is accentuated.

Spit sitting there if the semiotics

Is as is   silhouetted

repeatedly   yet he knows all this intersection

NOT-WRITING split sense from word

Backtracking

WRITING in book   annotating

NOT-WRITING in book   annotating a state of grace

A time to reap

NOT-WRITING the unsaid   to be found in quotients of index   poetics
more experienced

Incorrigible actuality all day. Wait a minute. Problems of   mind from
back to front:

A diet of

Nouns issuing from some few back pages of alphabetic   *pulsations and
values*

Not quite predicted through the strategic abstraction astonishing the
table

of contents up front

Rays and everything

Rewriting a stop

Is a pause such that

It need   not subsist on indemnity from unnameable   care

Hours minutes seconds rewriting the book inside out   rewritten.

Heretofore

The patent   went to the thief.

Disassembly   of onerous   share of fair share arousing Meucci   to our
time

To rewrite mere   fame

The erased trust

May I have a second of your timer. A time to reap   valor and sorrow.

More Weights

A. LET the record show speechless things thin speech being an assertion, let the recognition show *the reciprocal of this act*

B. if not, then a palpitating story reviving artisanal practices in extracting leaves and leave-taking writing their mirrors blindfold

C. time sensitive.   His phrase for it, page 338 sent each month along the dotted line. Open the window. He walked to the bakery to buy some bread. Power off, wait ten seconds

D. to each his own   within reach a fine mess   learning by doing, through experience

B. if not, then a palpitating story reviving artisanal practices in describing embarrassment, an embarrassment of leaves and leave-taking writing choral odes through the open blinds

C. time sensitive.   His phrase for it, page 338 sent each month along the dotted line. Open the window. He walked to the bakery to buy some bread. Power off, wait ten seconds. The refund is authorized

D. to each his own   within reach a fine mess   learning by doing, through experience owing to error's owning the decision.

A. Let the record show speechless things thin speech being an assertion let the recognition show *the reciprocal of this act* the ziggurat from which power startles

C. time sensitive.   His phrase for it, page 338 sent each month along the dotted line. Open the window. He walked to the battery to buy some bread. Power off, wait ten seconds The refund is ready and not-unplentiful although the caption has exaggerated the wholesome continuities therein of yeast's contingent, lopsided risen laughter

D. to each his own patience bringing roses within reach a fine mess learning by doing, by the same token through experience owing to error's owning the decision.

A. Let the record show speechless things thin speech being an assertion let the recognition show *the reciprocal of this act* the ziggurat from which power startles proem: if you had done all you could do and still could not effect change to the situation, then yes, there would be no hope; if, however,

B. by then a palpitating story's reviving artisanal practices in describing bespoke leaves rewriting their ions through the opening and closing slope of autumnal theater innocently administered to the windowsills

D. To each his own   bringing roses within reach a fine mess   not fast learning by doing nothing but not so indecisive to error.

A. Let the record show speechless things thin speech being an assertion let the recognition show *the reciprocal of this act* the ziggurat from which power startles proem: if you had done all you could do and still could not effect change to the situation, then yes, there would be no hope; if, however,

B. by then a palpitating story's reviving artisanal practices in describing kind and degree of leaves rewriting their ions through the opening and closing slope of commotion in flash autumnal shadow parts inaudibly loud

C. transactions along the dotted line. Open the window. He walked to the battery to buy some bread power. Off, wait ten seconds. An oration is plentifully from a woodcut. From a woodcut even as "WORLD" has risen, the orator has exaggerated the formula by simplifying it to a book from which wheat grows, therein to behold yeast's contingent, lopsided risen laughter.

Restlessness

Anticipating a bitter reproach are protocols to the rescue.

By a stroke of fortune, the journalist is sent far away; on leave to do, he promises opportunity to an understudy not at all reluctant to stay to be a counterpart and so better do the assignment.

Je ne sais quoi suffers indignities.

Just when he would have lost hope were protocols to the rescue.

By a stroke of fortune, the journalist is dispatched to a far shore; a lieutenant stays to do the assignment.

Je ne sais quoi suffers pangs' magnificent array.

Just when he would have lost hope—as, for instance, on page 283 (the paragraph next)—were resilient protocols to the rescue.

The journalist is sent away: from the flies, an understudy for hope.

Je ne sais quoi suffers pangs' magnificent array.

How many "its" can you find: "Can't the guy write?"

By a lucky break, when the journalist is dispatched to a far shore, an understudy, anticipating opportune nonsubservient life, stays to strike.

Je ne sais quoi suffers pangs' magnificent array.

How so? How ever?

An actuality small for his age holds an unpleasant eraser.

Dispatched to a far shore, a journalist; in his stead, an understudy.

Intrigue replenishes itself as, for instance, on page 283 (the paragraph next to last).

Je ne sais quoi suffers pangs' magnificent array.

An actuality small for his age holds an unpleasant eraser, diminishing returns optimized.

How so? Hindsight, forward-looking and prescient clouds in loud, ad hoc improvised and weighty topoi of sound standard ending decompose, desires your to-ings and fro-ings.

How many "its" can you find: "Can't the guy write?"

Jerk hindsight forward-looking and prescient cloudiness in loud ad hoc crowing, awfulness.

Request an equivocation or deferral or flat-out refusal or non sequitur or embattled intrigue's random subterranean equipment on the threshold's lost cause from the French.

Quest, small for his age

The protagonist is a fifth wheel irrelevant to the story trespass on some story that is solved without him.

The antagonist is a fifth wheel irrelevant to the story trespass on the story solved without you.

The referent—that imp—is but an apparition to the *spectator* (my emphasis) in adventure tantalizing and crumpled. A cause being humiliated is thereby giddily expressive rather than literally illustrative.

Chance, small for his age, anachronistic.

Jerk hindsight forward-looking and prescient cloudiness in loud ad hoc crowing, awfulness.

And then there was the gift: a bruise in panoply.

Insert premature hindsight forward looking and prescient rinceau ad hoc intrigue whereupon the bitter playmate at the standard ending is denied feast. The secret lies undisturbed on the unaccompanied stairway.

At the sibling feast the alleged protagonist, found unworthy, ostracized the referent.

To sustain itself an intrigue replenishes itself, as, for instance, on page 283, paragraph next to, which reads, "I promise you it would be distinct if it should dawn on you at all."

A lost cause small for his age.

And then there was the gift: a bruise in panoply.

Start over: a journalist offers the neophyte representation.

Start over unpleasantly.

I know what you're going to say.

Called away, a journalist leaves as another less-experienced self is called forth.

Feast or famine replenishes itself, as for instance on page 283.

And then there was the gift, a je ne sais quoi just below the ribs where she had fallen, fortunately. The misfortune lay elsewhere.

Opportunity, small for his age.

An *"alibi for voice"* is as though spontaneity were.

Jerk hindsight forward-looking and prescient cloudiness in loud, ad hoc crowing awfulness in awesome glare.

Don't interrupt me.

An "alibi for voice" is as though spontaneity were.

And there was the gift, a panoply just below where she had fallen, fortunately.

The misfortune lay elsewhere, as Aphrodite's mist left Menelaus looking ridiculous amid loud ad hoc crowing.

Insert premature hindsight forward-looking and prescient cloud, the ill humor permissible among familiars, meshed with indifferent monosyllables at the standard ending, denied feast not one moment too soon. Undisturbed on the interesting stairway is the impasse.

A person who cannot act but is merely acted upon is all-too-present to himself. The referent—that imp—is but an apparition to the *spectator* (my emphasis). Elsewhere a journalist is nonchalant about it.

Pervasive Spacing

—with Edmund Burke, James Mill, John Milton, and with Valentino Dixon

Sublime, Beautiful, Picturesque—*the nicest inquisition of the*
      Microscope

Is he developing his native tendencies? And where well-tended

Yours Sincerely is the courtesy to ask of twigs' instantiation
      or outcropping of niceties

having adroitness, unlike the denouement of the cairn or the nub of
      a keep

sheep near and far fairly close are uncropped rock and rough

irregular menu, the middle ground where humanity is said to reside

writing upon it disproportionate, and wept at that very moment against
      the struggling winds and roaring gales.

Scale: she was larger than the room in which she found herself.

We wrote earthworks' unsought emphasis

in detritus frequenting the kills raised to a park upon earth

more capable—what is the word for a lane in spring?—

metrics of walkways settling into its habitat momentarily

to and from moors' macroeconomies mentoring and the statement

wrought from it in pulchritude, which, having had its poet laureate

is leaping over, the frantic shade not impartial to wilderness

yet partial to postage stamps and securing the golf green's

consent the nub of crayons, not reading nature, reading himself

as it turned out quite the witness in kind. Seriousness

scanned promenade of contrast in the rough, roughly a source text

features to be deduced from neat sufficiency of dancing and French

tucked under the bodice, which let fall rustle and thence to induce wind winding golf for the incarcerated self.

                                        A gulf

shifted weight varying weighed timing of

ground drawn from postage wherein ampler

golf courses are, and so spirited he visited his grandmother and walked

free:

    "I know

it doesn't make sense but for some reason my spirit is attuned to it."

OR

Is he developing his native tendencies? And where well-tended
        yours sincerely

OR

A Modern Glacier

Point, Line, Plane step into a conjectural city nothing but

writing sideways sometimes the inverse of yellow

deletions. Undertaking clutter why do you not

cut, copy, paste the sought-for person

evading the New Wave simple-past change of heart

relatively. A concordance and a shame.

It may be dateless, John said. John said that

events are said to formula, similarly heuristic

to see her smile or to see her smile you took up the pencil's

calculus. At the crosswalk: yellow and resend. A sequence

opened that door. Without a mate during breeding time?

Whereby the achrony? Mary in analogue is played by entities

and oughts. Expedite the heart? Alms deprived of

once, once begun in momentum, nothing gets in the way of

abatement or as is, for instance. In medias res and so much comic

vestibule as per this and that: No, I do not need a rusted saw just yet,
      thank you.

In a conjectural city nothing but

writing sideways sometimes the inverse of yellow

deletions undertaking clutter traipsing across the New Wave

topos of Point, Line, Plane. Cut:

copy, paste the sought-for concordance

during breeding time. Why don't you

undo the digital yellow and resend the momentum

in the way of what-not ought?

As is, for instance. Very much and so much comic

abatement as per this and that No.

And resend the momentum

in the way of what-not ought

to be happening of that as per

Point, Line, Plane topos

or city writing the inverse of

as is, for instance.

Point, Line, Plane topos. Or city?

Memoranda

On the tide-flattened sand
strengthening
kelp and kelp from memory
kelp and kelp from memory slow dancing.

Black wet bestowed glass
white vinyl gray putty eraser

translucent synthetic rubber crumbling
underwater unanimity
opaque vinyl
putty

the nature of things.
The wet black bough

jumped murmur to elucidate
application questionnaire
invoice receipt ledger

journal that they have purgatory
on the tide-flattened sand faux-naïve with respect to objectively
        verifiable material
and some sort of gummy substance.

Some sort of gummy substance floating paraphrase
      on the tide-flattened sand.

Whereupon slow dancing eraser beige rubber translucent synthetic
      backspace

accelerating the fabula of simplification

as the better eraser or what the eraser has succeeded in

causing a skid, *a personally pen-signed*

or printed facsimile signature of a person with an enraptured

stamp a daybook for causing a surface of a person for a homecoming

to strike from afar yes to the ledger's feasibility study

as distinct from the magnifying glass that is the *wet black bough.*

The ledger's battle gear and its cause causing a skid

in retroversion for a tide-flattened surfeit

of a person reconciled itself to

white-gray vinyl breathed into a paragraph

a paragraph corporeal so it espouseth

erasure. A kind of writing in itself.

And which reconciled itself to counterproof breathed into

tide-flattened estimates, estimates tide-flattered

kinds: why the anapest beginning and ending

estuaries in and of flight the rising

testimony to wonder bright-edged

gifts beyond count?

Some Foreground

Statement unto treetops aphoristic: from whom do you think he got

Grammatical lamentations and counterweight? Long dominant
tolerance:

And admired are the creased verbs issuing in plentiful locutions

referring to his pioneering omissions at the periphery   Refer to reverb
for voice

"So what

Do you think of the garden?" "It's Abstract Expressionist," adjacent   as
a green   the unmowed   and

Realized at or near the condition of roving through the concept   to
leave out

Flowers is not to leave out roots, branches, leaves, the garden
reworded.

For the time being   decay eludes electronics   being

Specific to a chaos   and meanwhile I've loved *Canto V* too much of
undergrowth

Habitat's estranged gleaned glaring predicament.

Here is

Desert   for voice the explorer adores.

He later published vertigo tossed paint roller silage. The Situatonists

Are crushing Promethean char and happenings for voice and rubric.

As against the Sung

There: the periphery   gardenesque   to make a loud noise

Phrasal groundcover   a study in contrast verge   to make slow

Time to assist sentence not truth   but seasonal

Square doctrine had nest   to think over

Phrasal groundcover   a study in contrasts   verge   to make slow

Days for the tempestuous hedge   storytelling   grass to make

Saw-toothed statements   not meaning   allotted truth   come what
may

Nest   to make slow   ground cover   envy's next periphery

The truth to that nest's doctrine   make a circular square or market
square

Verging on received ideas   the mouth. The map's metalanguage   for
north

Detours are meaningful   slowly contoured gardenesque

Loud noise to allotments   giving rise to the edge's engrossing grass.

Tempestuous hedge   storytelling   to make a circular saw

Digressions are meaningful detours   to edges stubborn as a mule

Frustrated. Slow sentences gardenesque

Verge to come.

Brass Toy

Transfigured night
 at a tangent,
  the ardent edge
   of a triangular kind
   opus, knowing it
    throughout, below
     opening, the eye is
     fingering the
      opening shout
       convex holler
        endowment beveled
       a living quotient
       or plot or data
         cube of beveled air.
        It is night.

In this way   *and* for several *vine stocks*   listening even as ardently as
here   *lie unattended*   forgetful with absence and leaves   fingers spread
hypothetically in an encounter   with nutrients' inward way.   So that
fast tempi   conjoined with headlong rushing toward statement require
listening to the intrinsic   eras in stop-motion sample wrought alive   *so
that vines burst from my fingers*

. . . to him   translated *across the meaning-space*   that separates them.
Even so   little would give him the gist of it. *Points define   a periphery* or
contour   traversals pass   and yet the novice   may not.

Extract: vt. take out, esp. *by force; get by distillation, etc.; derive; quote*   n.
passage from book, film, etc.; concentrated solution   for it is as much as there
is and there is even a prosody for the coordinated gaps replete with fit
we take a lyric   to be sensible not lost to itself   in deposit of   thesaurus
with respect to

Points define
 Do not define; if not
  (may) define a contour
   Do not define a contour
    Even upon deletions, certainly
     Without deletions certainly
     Mark positions
      unmarked space
       Locating form
        Without location
        Yet also
         But not

If done reading   do not shelve / do shelve   put on table / leave   on table
near Will Call / put on table any   sorted / unsorted   to be sorted by /
not to be sorted until   graduate / closing   vine stocks and dots

Vine stocks omit *me fecit*   Unfit wheat behaves like leaves tasting of
preservative   no bread is eatable under the caterpillar   pattern does /
does not refer. Nutrients' inward way reviving stone's non-anonymity.   A
stone is a sentence is a site if you move it   if in rushing toward statement
it cracks market square. Wrought alive so that vines burst from my fingers
are baskets overwhelmed

Lyric: musical expressive subjective   lyric: musical expressive not
subjective   musical some expressiveness (as Boolean yes)   Lyrical
beauty not attractive not lovely not sweet not pleasant   lyric: musical
scan / not scan   Lyric: musical: scan / not-scan cadence

ADAMO

ME FECIT

In germ

Canto I, line 1,

E. P.'s

Handwriting

subjective not expressive (deckled) not (anonymously) musical

. . . a prosody for the nonwretched correlated gaps replete with forever-
including gorgeousness about. Someone asks: Is this Beauty? To which the
Netherlandish picture answered ostensibly: precise   empirically observed
yet unoccluded distribution of bright things in high polish. And stroking
a long sentence and having no quarrel with opulence through lapidary
saying   relative to which that scant posit in few syllables left of who-
knows-what? may be as much surviving the foregone in memoriam   we
are not mentioning that language was not lost to those who spoke / wrote
it obnoxiously from a thicket. The dialect of Madder Lake

does not fade   does with white admixture. Apples and / or oranges this
modernity (owned by John Maynard Keynes). In an arc of claimants   is
the central apple   now to pivot from belonging. And so on   required of
red (recovered) matter-of-factly featureless species does feature   strokes
to the set   attendant to golden not in the least although just enough to
count   non-red for green And:

proverbially. And here a thoroughly analytic phrase-upon-phrase to open
infinity. Infinite? Or finitely large   photography? Vine stocks and dots
left unattended And: to be enumerated: precise bright distributions
in high polish not so empirical   as compared with precise fixative of
the accidental double exposure of extra who-knows–what? Exploding
languages? *Pound's dots,* she sd. So that: the eloquence of the fissure
precipitous not indecisive   and as to futurity replete with Who goeth or
oranges. The colon: its rhetoric puts   necessity to the ideology *when you
come to the gates of Go*   of expulsion if not exile   to which statelessness
we submit our credentials. Go minus Stay absolutely   but really the

portal Go   by ADAMO. Visit round green rind *blue like an orange* pointing
takes up previous next   does not fade   takes low-hanging

transfigured night
 fishtailed mesh
  at tangent to archaic
   rind substituting up
    of stray exile
     far below infinity's
      plotless marshy opus wherein
       ardent iris cut quagmire.
      It is modern night.
     No fixed abode
      a stimulant for some
       all none bull roarer's
        torn negative
         vertices as if to say:

outburst of vine stocks by (close to / by means of) campaign knee-
deep in hindsight pulsed birth sex death actuarials the thrush brought. If
compared with Still Life what sentence goeth? Imprecise nonexpressive
forever of bright things in high polish retaining very little opulence except
through lapidary   sayings are these seven apples.

Clear and distinct   nonpejorative negative still life when you come to the
gates of   Go   focus   plot   mud-encrusted knowing formless
[   ] to be an alloy   settlement set on horseback stratified
aftermath entailing sentences   exhaling ellipses   apostrophe intact
exhaling. Bas-relief of contending mesh. Beveled exit also belongs to the
entrance cut through portal's circularity in the scholars' garden much vista
at each step   up nonidentical of the same fleeing stop as shallow serial
stepping portends verticality as charged. See also wire rope   suspension
over water   river over river burst from my fingers red and black sea-
surge some submerged clusters red blue green whose axis   at dusk
accomplished nonfinite space between integers   the real aporia also
engulfed because   expulsed. Alternatively   a noncontradictory reading

of periphery may well entail the known a priori indicating that this
species spelt in the gaps   is coherent with scheme and script: you apart /
together   the grid necessary to all lyric

entailment: musical some *penseroso* blazon percussive over what smears
apart together apart together   entailment: musical blazon percussive over
what *penseroso*   neither omission nor deletion nor possibly reduction but
rather a segmental arc oscillating   nomenclature melancholic put to affect
the pictorial doctrine such that even where incomplete—who what where
when why peripatetic   throbs where and how   *penseroso* transferred to
Benjamin's pondering pentimenti. Affect yet not form.   Lyric entailment:
musical blazon percussive   sound blocks   agon   there and then to
ellipses from which issues omission   making verifiable noise to raise our
eyes from the expulsed. Full stops trail off

   come forth. Everywhere floated that year in cinema   lately indefinite
furlough doubtful perhaps blur with ethically mute insinuations   as here
a deficiency inaudible to oneself no more fresh or efficacious attributed
to seem not now   minus then atmospheric somewhere to which middle
distance is that very past perfect.

They   a farrago of gray areas   staying   affix go to gray areas   seriously.
He smoothed a fresh page of stay and go   all of both. Stay and not.
Suppose that Pound's dots conjoining harrowing logic to field notes swung
together as one AB   harvested luxuriant delay from this less obtrusive
circumstance. As they speak ellipses conjugating limbs intertwined   tree-
structure Not both stop-and-go   *though of course there can be duplicated
as when . . . accomplish as identical action they are syntactically speaking
one . . .* event or of change   decipherable? Knots mental diagram thy
revolution: we sing of the corrective's punctual strenuousness of that   glut
of late. Late ellipses flush with an unrepaired periphery inherited a lunatic
distinguishing himself at the premature gate of must stay all must and
must not. All stay and all go   imagine a formless infinity   undid said
intention by this when complexity is meant vine stocks' and Bach's. But
admit that. . . . maintaining a formless infinity nonmelodically under and
over the matrix   remains a stray   math. Pass plotless handfuls of a yet

different any   algebra almost as much so frequented as   speech itself
ellipses not impressive to cultivated watchful   with open eyes quotient
of walks intersecting with self-exile after abducting her excursion   out
strolling to refresh a stay. Dichotomies lie unattended.

Calm unpainted
 And bulk windswept
  Load-bearing densities
  Seized bas-relief
   Yawn painted black
   At least oblique
    As that short crux
      Throughout advent's reverse
      Ripple extruded
      Vine providing that
      Accordion being
      In parallel housing.
       An ardent individual
        Surfaces. It is night
        With objects.

ENTER

Adjacent entries in nonadjacent sense   poetics of

To and from joy increasing

Speech speed   paradise paranoia

Rewriting an existing home   *nouveau roman* **odyssey**

"agglutinative" syntax

Singing

A sepulchral epigram

dictes and sayings of   a refrain's worth

Of space-time annuity is pointing to the film   the film's coating

Iron oxide run through a ring and be erased   text.

Would you?   M. W.: "Do you worry

About the degradation of

your tapes?"

C. C.: "All the time."

A Complex Sentence

1.

The less labor, the more spur

the manuscript submitted   lengthier
the manuscript submitted   not lengthier.

Soft thump
against which

memory's
soft thumps against incident

Unfamiliarity
arouses curiosity

repeated
flannel

thumps against glass

against glass
obstruction

to shelf swing
within

sight

System departed

from skills already to go; at hand
bird battering itself

while   not-writing staring down holding pen even
at the sumptuous computer   standing up pacing   turbulence
then returning with the thought to type it

Not-looking at   muse   humanistic   does not impede a quick
manslaughter   thought all at once in a rush
of   return carriage press ENTER space bar   transposing letters
and introducing extra letters wrong proximate keys
substitutions   S + 7   missing
missed incipient spaces
of eternal present and grace   grace even so easy   of revision
nonlaborious   what do I think of this

thought taking in   interim worry for ruminative objection you yourself
state silently knotted
and re: Pierre Boulez   his retaliating alternative nemesis having left
for frequency density intensity   with the help of perturbations
and conflict re: Boulez
A pair of entropies   devoted   to a complex sentence
The perturbations which change its structure represent so many
negations of this existence parted.

Game matrix
which he confided as IRCAM had newly begun
had newly begun "to read and write all over, again like a child," he had
said to us
The more labor, the more spur

In the always fresh
saying

Then his saying
"the most elusive"

to fabricate   is the flesh of   timbre decaying
lit   up lap lit lip list   hat brim

repair

like new   the page in grace
a leaf perpetually thought ear's rehab
thought's stamina for
DELETE

CUT PASTE MOVE SAVE samba for memory routines

Action the alphanumeric and
frequency in retrieval with retrieval in silk
knotted metric.

Removing shelf
let bird cease.

System departed.

2.

The more labor, the less spur

In the philosophy of science
learning the operating system met with resistance
from the student at the keyboard for whom enmeshed efficacy
had probability. To be in synch for now mere know-how will do it
please
the more routine the better   keystrokes for the algorithms most like
that of the routine task transferred from obsolescence. But what an
idea!   A cause for wonder
is this mind in zeros and ones adding to inestimable cultural magnitude
possessed of detritus   the lost

Being abstract
departed from the tabula rasa
even at the sumptuous computer   the muse standing up pacing   spacing
noise   then returning with the thought to type it

Not-looking at   typographical error does not sever a quick   thought all
at once in a rush
of focus   return carriage press ENTER space bar   transposing letters
introducing extra
horns in the brass   section of zinc additive
difficulty ruminative awake once more you yourself state

Learning to write   again yet not in all   function flourishing
familiarity
Now I can learn the system.

SELECT
familiarity as though typing on the typewriter minus soft controls
hard   ware

Missing   the shoulder-action the mechanics the sounds   supporting
the movement of SHIFT   Wish granted. Wish for DELETE INSERT   CUT
PASTE
sight from screen to keyboard to screen   puts a strain on   and so
squinting to read roe ad dial
dilating to write. More errors' dim glare   lit lap lit lip list   hat over eyes

30,000 lines in retrieval   metrics intricately knotted   restored in silk the
design of vivacious will's schematic contours   and at the controls

Sounding   again yet not in all   function flouncing

in anticipating objections. His was the duologue as it did sound
the readers' resistance to algorithm therein. So then this teaches *how
to think, not what to think.*
Set to éclat
Boulez wrote

Or starts to:
Key functions most close to those of the vibrant typewriter   then key a
heuristic from which

electronic intimations
without the lugubrious recopy   brought about the perpetual renewal of
fair copy.
[Change "editing, but in" to "editing, but for" estate
selected "And, so," delete; capitalize "b."]

Ease has its consequences in facility. An editor tells me that since the
advent of computer technologies, fiction manuscripts have increased in
length, by twice at least, as writers have no incentive to be economical
in thought.
[Delete opening clause "With this, we cannot commit to memory (so
readily)"; change "as" to "As"; capitalize "A"; change "writing. A" to "as"
in lower case "a"; change "halves halve"; delete "haves."]

Sonics   even animals   if you had to name the string.

Random-access memory   speak to me

The less labor   the more length
prolix
The less labor   the same length
profligate

over-coding the ordinary pounding
here and there
to be erased of course   except in memory

The soft thumps
Saying

"Timbre, the most elusive."

In a screen's dim glare
nomenclature   is not you.
We Speak Nomenclature

Set to short shrift that a not-unintelligible exegesis
enters this knotted wall   several few many all
who speak   the abatement
of   sounding
a
resistance   reluctance
in not-unintelligible concrete labor   not-more algorithm thereupon
shelf or plateau
of shelf therefore in core commands most like
known prior labor thereto.

Put
reprieve
beside me   later odes
by revising a short manuscript already at hand
not only there and further
ease.

The more labor the more spur   and branching out from that
emergent and emitted interpretive flexing
having been pent up in author's substrate
and prolix comb.

Prolepsis Photobooth

In some world
the prologue has reprisal
most fully one, two, three   nonpareil anticipation.
And answering   did I write that?   Sparse   then.
Being ahistorical   is a ways off
replenished with each latency   eternal
statement   we remember   against which
the next time will have come
coming to term—renaming latency she always arrives
minutes late   meaning she herself
is replenished   nonpareil perennially
unfazed out of phase in kind. Days
later we remember that. She arrives, always late
"always"   said for emphasis   or if for stamina   needful
sparely. Sparse rather   would be very small abundance
page 66   excerpted from forever and a day.

Being ahistorical myth is a ways off
replenished with each forever   and is stamina.
In some world one, two, three   nonpareil
agency and answering   abundance.

One, two, three   nonpareil.

Birdsong

Subbituminous   cause and effect

As charcoal   memory annealed to commentary,
gather a few phrasal things

gathering a few phrasal   things
And key terms   anthracite   brain is there
is there with the knight's request   for a periodical

Subbituminous   cause and
as charcoal
gather a few diaristic things

. . . to gather clutter
And key terms   anthracite   brain

As charcoal, we
gather a few clumps   journals and photos

. . . to gather a few drenched knights
And key terms   anthracite

Codex under these from subbituminous
cause in burial.

I, at Fault

> *Let death and exile, and all other things which appear terrible,*
> *be daily before your eyes, but death chiefly; and you will never*
> *entertain any abject thought, nor too eagerly covet anything.*
> *Demand not that events should happen as you wish; but wish*
> *them to happen as they do happen, and your life will be serene.*

Epictetus

1.

in the hands divinities,
shepherd to have through mute
early earthly

Are fond. Depicted,
deletion portrayed as

, **for a thing which is a credit** thunderous distress
Alignment Consummation,   **To be unworthy**
Of continuity   From **being** snakebitten   death
Certain **peremptory** eventful

instantaneous notably **cut**   divergent
Again
Accomplishment   immortal pairing
stirs   chooses

Red-and-green demonstrative
Fore grand background mountain in sky
Earth in the hands, mortality of the flawless
Snakebite. Above and below we read as why
Transposed, transmuted shepherd to have
A snake draw stoically from sound

Principles and modal color schemes lost
On most of you.

                  Lost-and-found flaw
In love with a mortal, inconspicuous
On purpose reads as naturally put
Portrayal although it is not. If distinct
Otherwise, neither is it expressiveness.
Nor is it nothing. Nor is it a sentence.

draw stoically
On most of you.

                  Lost-and-found flaw
In love

Of continuity is worth. From **being**
riverbeds' inferential
Alternative spaces underneath

            then will do for

        and now and wherefore
Ungrounded unto him undone, undoing

Again of such-and-such agnostic

, anything S depicted by P
Creature to a fault, frantic thunder,
Much more disturbance than this something
I conclude

2.

                    To be unworthy
Of continuity is worth.

Open hello, as color. Spatiotemporal
Earth and sky, sky and earth elsewhere
Tumbling raw and cooked blades
Of lightning, for a thing that is algebra
Symptomatic of the inauspicious
Bite, fruitful obviously, in all one thought
Folded in half from being metope snakebitten,
Certain peremptory mountains and faults

Cascading, forests and livestreaming
Winds and riverbeds' inferential
Alternative spaces underneath
might be can then will do for you to
Divulge musculature in a cleft's
Righteousness or loveliness.

            in   **not to**

notably cut   **not for nothing**

Is earth aghast

We, a translation
Again of such-and-such agnostic
Edges

or not to.

announces she
In shadow all too frequently
surely
                    we are. We

proverbial waxing

And waning general criteria
to the urn and its sung configuration.
Interred is

is earth before
Reveal.   By which

                    flawless
One because absent.
                              At the eye
And matter
The Burial

Of marked unmarked
          Earth sky
                    Beauties and blanks

To forego the

                    City in the distance

3.

Rhyme
      premature   netherworld distraught
Evermore
Scratches in disarray and

I, intertextual, anything S depicted by P.
Inscribed, the rustics converge. What mortal
R of faith clearing delete and subtitle
cut itself on shadow, the said finger of
Which got the idea, initially at least,
From inevitable realities in the sky's
Overflowing banks of blue-and-green
Cloth, of a statement bestowed upon
A cloud.
               Here and there flashes of N.
A discussion is in progress. *It was not*
Darkness that fell from the air. It was
Brightness. The time is now. Humans
Require distinct oxygen. Otherwise
We died from being entablature. CAUTION.

      knew

P looking at and being

         Evermore becoming the split
Sky

   left out: see
               fortune

Accomplishing a Humanism, 2015

T my name is techne and my husband's name is temple. We come from
    theory and we sell time lag.

In the name of mind is a tacit enclosure to put the rift. We come from
    the "theoretic intellect" within.

We come to contemplation through implements. An incision made
    the brainstorm.

We come from above the eyes and below the ears, timpani we are
    no longer speaking of.

Themselves, a collapsible dwelling for the mouth withdrawn: here the
    long tongs' spring action. For that then I am at the departure
    gate awaiting

eventfulness. The temple sells time lag; "lag time" is a theatrical term.
    And howsoever rainfall

will wend its way, consecrating the hydrograph, its "heavy scent" of
    ascending and descending,

he thought of techne too late, had a mortal compensating for the eve

to come, tomorrow the sacred error we come from, thoroughly
    looking at

time lag. T my name is techne frequently and here is a tally of
    themselves in lengthily

indicated kind.

T my name is making or doing and my husband's name is sanctuary. We
    come from speculation

and we sell delay now since, throwing some shade on Leonardo. My
    name is to come

and my husband is he who befalls a space. We are taught something
    that touches a curve

were beauties accepted or proved as a theory. Its small timbering
    beholds

an undertaking come to emergent thought from a thirst in that

Athena. Of many things and many endeavors, my name is techne

bent in and out for attempting the arts of that thesaurus being so
dearest.

And my husband's name is Atlantis, a male figure used like a caryatid

to support an idea, accepted column, or pilaster. We come from far off

and we sell tendency. Artisanal market is my name and my husband's
name is a space.

We come from an ideal set of facts, principles, and conditions associated
together

at that time, soon after. Where or when, my name is held in the hand

and my husband's name observes treble auguries where we come from.

As if, often viewed negatively.

His is sacred-because-not-for-sale, mine is through-thick-and-thin.

We come from allowing-that and we sell timetables. Optimistic

arrival although it may be, tarmac no farther than touchdown

is our unhappy thoroughfare thrown off on a tangent

until against and athwart extreme theater-in-the-round.

Theta rhythm does not like annuities deferred to not-now.

Heart-ache, touch-me-not. So what is the design flaw?

I changed the artisan, who did not hesitate beneath premonition:

without prong, the buckle becomes the means by which the strap
loosens

lengthening as the wearer walks. Stray threads

given sanctuary for episteme, a space marked off ably thermal,

seem to wend our way. Extempore to help people, an idea waited.

The bag left techne stranded

Moreover, this was a kind of thingamabob: why this? Without prong

again, to wend our way the strap loosens, lengthening as you,

the wearer, saying "Stay, stray threads, stay with me"—but with VAT,

and why this tax on love? Soon after I wondered that

intestate appearing to promise pensive timetables and thoroughly long

sanctuaries for episteme, a space marked off for mindful

trial. We come to theorems, appearing to these and as much song

from the sky to the ground sliding through and through

the apparatus as it remains without weighted contents

of a person's use. Theory enters, techne exits: the untested longing

trying esteem, a template, and then some fine-textured spilling

use elsewhere as may be inferred from such untimely longing longer

mortal entity unkempt in the polis,

thereafter a thickness.

Drawing Lots

And too soon, eftsoon lawn daisy untimely

Skald despoiler plagiarist last in first

Sledgehammer set uppermost Wild Oats (a place-name)

Through which he-who-exerts-himself utterly

Urges furrowing on behalf of our terrible species,

Of which forensic scant hope, says he of the yardstick.

And too soon, eftsoon lawn daisy timely

Loop-on-thread last in first

Sledgehammer the red uppermost

Rack of seaweed like a difficult skald

Through which he-who-exerts-himself utterly

Saith the word for he-who-would-shape-his vowels-carefully.

Everything I Look On

Go
Life
and All. Where   do signs of life first appear? Let us avail ourselves of "By
the road   to the contagious hospital"   wherein readers almost always
miss   the stop
Color

Green green green green, the four-color problem

The office is open during business hours; the showroom by appointment
only
      verdure
not visible from the street behind the showroom   the office is open. Go
there. The office and showroom are always open; just ring the bell. Access
to the basement through the showroom requires that from the office
comes someone to the door to let you in.
May I post a notice on the door to this effect?
No "yes, buts"
      verdure
leafage   pasture sod turf   for the office not visible
  but ramified   shade   open but off
      wide of the mark
wild glass flashing
      the lyric extremity   signs of

Trespass welcome   crossing the sustainable threshold   stop   the public
green   open to the air and accessible to the senses   hours of operation
during daylight favor red but toward dusk   green appears brilliant and
note that 2%   dark blue   the primaries as far as the eye can see limits
for either an indeterminate gate with a biological necessity
or the little   office
      grue
staring back   knowingly
blue darker under the same light as red it has been written   iris by
whose authority

to open literally but closed now or closing no or closing down apparatus
accessible always   open but by appointment for a field operation or opera
off-limits   what if   quite visible
from the street
          closing down
rough moss

and sustaining a flesh wound. Pigment subtractive to black upon mixture
of red green yellow blue orange purple go stop bruise under construction
provoked both / and   ax to grind hospitality throughout green oxide   let
us wield a tincture of red ramifying the indeterminate field of dye quite
literally waiting for a green light
    have you received a facsimile
of celadon it
          stains

Ferric to ferrous pause   drop temperature   aperture of celadon
singularly a pause as eyes replay go but off-limits and initial it   clement
remedy usually edible herbage   youthful vigorous green not ripe or
matured   field factory office showroom   fresh tender factory showroom
by appointment freshly sawed not   aged unseasoned   eventfulness in
vitrines and / or downstairs screening with discussion for any profusion
you have
          waste greenish
overripe and plenty of death
received dyed green   seasoned then   or greenish mess beyond celadon
jade leave this
stop open closed welcome eventful craquelure fresh-faced of the reduced
atmosphere.
Tender kiln, initial it.

In slate sea   Klangfarben may occupy the same similar congruent
iteration oxidating
    mucous light   arterial dark-bright contagion of which we are
          Verdure virulent   overripe   odor
gunmetal to go
          apple off limits
or inaccessibly tempting within the vitrine of display   are daring
instruments the vitality of which flashing   glass OPEN BUT OFF-LIMITS
VACANCY NO   GO concerning it   slate shades of open   I am mindful
with discussion for any profusion aged   mold moldering and eventful
pastures lavishly indeterminate Go

       verdigris shards of
olive bread versus a priori green
       and notating photons
flashing green modem ON or sure   and snap Go To launch daylight hours
of logic the same square and union whose vertices   verdure electric as
brightness: The office is open during business hours; the showroom by
appointment only

Old English *gan* "to advance, walk; depart, go away; happen, take place;
conquer; observe, practice, exercise," from Germanic **gaian* (cognates:
Old Saxon, Old Frisian *gan,* Middle Dutch *gaen,* Dutch *gaan,* Old High
German *gan,* German *gehen*), from PIE **ghe-* "to release, let go" (cognates:
Sanskrit *jihite* "goes away," Greek *kikhano* "I reach, meet with"), but there
does not seem to be general agreement on a list of cognates.

       shards of appled
gates

May I post a notice on the door to this effect? Hours of operation are
inaccessible or speculative   a mind open without authorization to open
the message   to get "the green light"; unless one can view the why and
the wherefore   practicality remains indeterminate or wild   evergreen
bacterial   pause to scrub from Go
   in verdure teeming
with green   life   always open; just ring the bell.

Commemorative Onset

READING:

MOSTLY OBELISK   THE LEAST OBELISK
BAS-RELIEF   STOPPAGES

BAS-RELIEF AND STOPPAGES
BAS-RELIEF OR STOPPAGES
NO BAS-RELIEF AND STOPPAGES
NO BAS-RELIEF OR STOPPAGES
MOST BAS-RELIEF AND STOPPAGES   BAS-RELIEF STOPPAGES
LEAST BAS-RELIEF AND STOPPAGES
LEAST BAS-RELIEF AND STOPPAGES   STOPPAGES

bas-relief and obliged stoppages
obliged / not obliged—but that is another regime
mostly obelisk
distributed throughout the bas-relief—but that
is another regime
The most bas-relief with the least stoppages
or stop acres—but that   provident

in bas-relief
belongs to the most stoppage.

MOSTLY OBELISK   THE LEAST OBELISK
BAS-RELIEF   STOPPAGES

Not in the least
glare
belonging to leisurely bas-relief itself
belonging to most if not all and then some great
even greater than the sum of its parts
and art long attaining to experience expressly effortful lifetime
almost a maxim extremely the most obelisk

and cause
achieving greatness long-lived and if anything on the increase more
and more might   with strength ascribed to
having prevailed sound strong and considerable parchment
in the zenith whose altitude has been noted
extensively serious and host to many a windswept stoppage
as sad as it is intense
lavish whacking

Life is short BAS-RELIEF

OR STOPPAGES REMAIN MOSTLY
and art long   ALL UNION BELONGING TO
BAS-RELIEF AND STOPPAGES
NO RELIEF AND opportunity fleeting,
experience perilous   NEITHER BAS-RELIEF NOR STOPPAGES TOUCH
and decision difficult. THAT BAS-RELIEF–INTERSECT
PROVIDENT AND
LEAST

LESSER
ADJACENCY
NO RELIEF AND NO experience
LESS PURPLE and art long NOT PROVIDED WITH
ANY PATHOS COMPANION TO
life short   impossible—
and art long   improbably belonging to having had
read
much prodigy into it.

. . . finish what you have started: leave the city at long last. The gates are open: go.

—Cicero

Seated in the vernacular
Not seated at the vernacular
Unseated   with shades drawn.

Seated in the vernacular   with shades drawn not to
forget and in virtue of   Not seated at short notice
with as if   vernacular   Unseated with shades
drawing a boast fading into a threat to the depth of

Seated and drawn to being routed is a prompt
to earthworks   not to forget errands or circuits'
vernacular fire   escapes nor stairs nor elevators nor
landings splashed with stains and   baggage   some
carefree   arrest is not a questionnaire but may be a
survey from   whence   and as to whether   sharing
night train's delay with shades drawn. Seated but routed
interrupted by a decision not a mood yet with a few ions
and to a depth   of the page past due. Acting alone is not
self-evident   you yourself seated with shade   drawn and
frequently not a deterrent to standing up. A boast fading
into glaring shade

Seated in the vernacular   earthwork the most the
least none   some shade pulled across the decision   of a
perceiving subject

Not being seated surrounded the idiom of the light
switch. Being seated as a percentage   in sheets stapled
with sparks for which you yourself the ersatz conduit
but pointedly   have   tested the conduit's telling
defects' lopsided timbre   what constitutes the circadian
electronics.

Some lights any shade pulled across an immensely useful subject

Unseated in the studio: to the depth charge on short notice—Watch out! Earthworks are waking   without statuary in a seated position but not without sacrifice glancing off seizures in the   round   one's descant   the moving edge of modernity in the red box   modernization not in the red box   modernism in the blue box.

Not seated at short notice with shades pleased as if unseated with undersaturated shades drawn down a boast fading into a threat to the depth of   being seated as a percentage   in sheets stapled   with sparks for which you yourself the ersatz conduit but pointedly   Seated in the vernacular   Not seated at the vernacular   Unseated   with shades drawn plus slide   in disfavor escalating idiom of the informality at large in the polis   slang attire   practically everyone wearing cross talk   and vagueness

Unsated in the studio: to the depth charge on short notice— Watch out! Upon waking without statuary   in a seated position and without reliquary surrounded and memorial   a prompt to colloquial earthworks not to forget errands   circuits to be interrupted by a decision not in the mood for intelligence answerable until no more. Acting alone is not self-evident   you yourself seated by the fire in Descartes's dressing gown   with shades drawn and frequently not a deterrent to standing up. A boast of earthworks fading into unplace glancing off seizures in the round   cannot but have heard   the moving edge of modernity in the red box   modernization not in the red box modernism in the blue box.

Not-and statuary desktop tabletop reliquary. The moving edge of the non-empty you of years   making the sacrifice to intelligence   the moving edge of studio and action stemming therefrom.

A boast fading into a glaring forfeit surrounded the idiom of the light switch. Being seated as a percentage to benevolence of averages stapled with sparks for which you yourself the ersatz conduit but pointedly   have

tested the conduit's telling defects' lopsided timbre   what constitutes
the circadian electronics. Seated and surrounded studio hands exactly so
provided that motet blended as if. The moving edge of the non-empty you
of years   making the sacrifice to intelligence   the moving edge of studio
and action stemming therefrom. At short notice we settled just behind
the sunrise in arrest otherwise seized stunned handed over. Therefore
unseated.

In truth: on short notice—Watch out! without statuary   in a sated prompt
to colloquial earthworks not to forget errands   circuits to be interrupted
by a motet glancing off seizures in the round threat or depth charge   one's
descant   the moving edge of modernity   in the red and not seated

      without motet glancing off seizures   in the round modernity

      the vernacular seated not seated.

        In the round   we the vernacular seated not seated.

          Not seated.

          Reading otherwise.
          Reading sometimes.
          Not reading.

        Reading otherwise provided that   lamp
        Reading sometimes provided with   two
        approaches directives extant   Reading otherwise
        provided that angles jiving give orant-splayed
        protocols some panache

        Reading   provided that   light   reading provided
        with no light   reading or light   reading provided with
        approaches artificial or natural reading provided that
        no lackluster approaches   diffused is best   reading
        provided that only artificial light very much less   and
        abaxial and yet onto page   reading provided with light

minus loquacious light any   reading provided with
artificial light some   some affinity

delights. Reading or light   reading and light delights and
instructs   reading directives instructs   not delights
all reading directions or reading directions to orient
trenchant assembly   belonging to extant fragments from
posthumous directives. To orient assembly is to bestow
wealth on extant fragments. Any reading all

otherwise rereading menus   or reading not any   or
reading menus provided that variable diasporic page.
Attrition of not reading   and jiving and splayed and
protocols   for splayed menu—not table—with orant-
splayed protocols   angles menu with jiving orant-splayed
protocols provident not stinting angles jiving orant-
splayed protocols some panache.

Reading otherwise diaspora   French menu extant from a
vast array of sudden angles emits a style. Hot parenthesis
wet and cold parenthesis   hot and cold parenthesis wet
and dry parenthesis   French menus of 1916 in New York.

Reading   provided that   light   reading provided with
no light reading or light only   No lackluster reading
provided with light artificial or light natural   reading
provided that only natural light—diffused is best. Other
than this   reading lamp and not track lighting and not
wall washers' extraneous glare abundantly deluxe. Dim
deluxe calm. And not facedown. Face   down with fingers
shielded from the shade drawn and provident   is reading
provided with no flood   yet with awe reading   any open
book   no book or just one lemony flood abundantly.
Reading no flood yield. Not-and flood track wall. Then
again light provided that   lamp provided that bulb
provided that filament did not: change bulb. Reading
more heat than light: change lamp. Acquire extant supply
of light. Provident lamp reads opening. Reading and
belonging to it provided that artificial light very much less
and abaxial and yet onto page   reading provided with

light any or reading provided with daylight some   some
affinity

Reading otherwise provided halt yet with sentences   pause a
failure that strikes waiting for forethought   yet with a remainder
provided with cessation of rain neon thread a permissible
derivative revolutionary then again off and on   as a drawstring
breathes an arrondissement of thread   and filament   *filament out
of itself.* Otherwise not raining   songs.

Stay reading: sometimes provided with reset   extant go continue
stay with cant   a fair copy   provided that furlough or contour
mostly a frieze in   anthologies' implicit argument   and vocation
where to   where off at the rate of encroachment   and stay
warfare styles of

Not reading songs otherwise from the perspective of the
vanquished   approaches cant without gate and yet with
alterations   to future a priori teeth   portcullis very much subject
to vigorous heat.

Reading *very much what they would do as a decision.* At the logic gate strong
enough and somewhat very much canted   *stories documents bits of poetry
hymns mnemonic devices* intestate but rebuilt from within they were bound
to follow help from readers to destroy   unscrew.

Stay reading very much   what they would do as a decision up to and
including expansion—always expansion—why not canted from within
why cant gate how to make a decision how not   why not stories ready
stories but not documents reading none of these   reading no stories
but documents   reading neither stories nor documents sometimes
reading neither stores nor offices nor traffic gate on the hill   gate with
wherewithal belonging to mnemonic devices   a keep   stories and
documents with bits of poetry or hymns   documents municipal and
documents institutional   encroachment where upon intestate or settled
not settled in very much but not any interpreted estate with poetry
reading rebuilt from within to extend domain without   not rebuilt from
within and rebuilt their own not with their own with our nice screwdriver

screw and hatchet not fish fork   not-and fish fork screw not-or hatchet
not any tools any and all instruments provided that army knife.

Not reading treasury   of the word provided with if then bas-relief from
which you yourself construe on off encryption that moves axial behaviors
to ruddy eventfulness. Equip teeth and blades past and future   friction
how to and how not often otherwise from the perspective of the   circuit
breaker   this happens then that environs which dictate aphorisms from
within adverse redaction   breakage   not to refrain   to do to stay a
waiting list for things done well. Stop. Go must be done definitely   the
broad bowl well regulated as infill   complaints are not yet trenchant
grievances nor   a suitable true / false

In truth: not-reading otherwise provident page provided halt yet with
French diasporic   filament of itself in menus   *au courant* orant-splayed
in pause that strikes waiting for forethought   yet with a remainder
provided with cessation of rain neon thread a permissible derivative
revolutionary then again off

     and on   reading otherwise   provident provided halt   and
     diasporic menu with cessation of artificial light some   some affinity.

          Reading diaspora otherwise provided halt with artificial
          light   some.

          Reading otherwise.

          Walking as if cursively
          Walking apart discursively a shelf
          Walking that pamphlet.

          Walking as if   cursively even when not
          Walking although past due   not cursively but as a
          kind of discrete series   Walking that pamphlet

Walking as is   cursively even when not walking as is
and walking as is unlike a centaur and unlike a centurion
and unlike taking the first essential step   in rhythm by
instinct or by practice or insofar as practice becomes
economics with sundries plausibly   and as though on
a walking tour and wearing a sundial lost sunglasses
coordinated and keeping pace with the pavement   to
sustain a frequency   or mechanism thereof or otherwise
performing a task that could be performed by other
people (voluntarily performed or in physiological
memory)   how acquired or how retained memory (how
acquired then how not retained) memory how retained
sundial   not-and with sundries and lost umbrella   not
lost   found sunglasses a found ready-made comb or
some wild fibula something that if held in the hand incises
as he did   for incising leather said the leather maker: was
it not? Is.

Walking although past due   not cursively but as a kind of
discrete series / with others   with any almost everyone
five others   in single file to avoid oncoming to and fro
second row fourth from left center mezzanine   not-and
the center (and railing obstructed and view pitched)
late: a statement and making a statement about belonging
to himself not they whom he would visit   and missed
themselves with all but a delay on the tarmac or flying
in to arrival only not yet   keeping pace with conjecture
minus the gate   the without   gate away from apart not
yet at or on

Walking that pamphlet   begat more plight pitch and
strait not so well regulated as ordinary and also composed
to a purpose of the everyday (physiological or voluntarily
performed) iterated from language as of as if cursively
as he wrote lyric dramatic epic notwithstanding in
circulating blood or in handwriting not-and in circulating
blood but in sentences. He walked in sentences. True.

Walking apart discursively deliberately   reset foot from
pamphlet not-unrestricted respite from conjecture   allocating
foot to pavement or to shelf any   means (not and any or none)
but a means belonging to some corridor (no hall or stadia)
some   hall of flexible size to make way to and from a place.
Not any corridor in vehemence please no house beautiful. No?
Nonsense at least   a maze to say a self-interfering corridor   a
loop recursively   as is   yet unbound steady corridor resuscitates
edge: cue to assumptions in favor or disfavor   apart discursively
a shelf for digressions past due scenic and excessively blessed and
about hands off.

As if walking yet unbound   conjecture past due ramp and stair
amped up rolling   escalator as a kind of discrete series of forming
an opinion when a process called for steadfast edge in favor or
disfavor for a discursive search not spendthrift shelf digressive
unauthorized any. As if walking past addenda.

Reset walking a value in itself to stations' other algorithm   not
cursive   equal to impress   but better impressed edge with
discrete series   hook and eye lock coats bags traveling   what
constitutes favor or disfavor's torn scrap of firmament   scaled to
an inscription   this and earth   of that

Reset walking a value   in itself   to impress none someone
everyone   equal to impress but better with   a pamphlet of value
(*quality of being useful or desirable*): queue eyewitness feather
duster for instance   best in favor (*a kind helpful acknowledgment
and a strong lasting impression*) edge with hook and eye socket a
lock for coats bags traveling what constitutes favor or disfavor's
torn scrap of firmament   scaled to an inscription   this and earth
of that

. . . walking that pamphlet as if cursively provident   And recursively not
a villa not a settlement on horseback and or not a scavenger's periplum—
see that tree? Not from here indexical where   once was a homestead
meaning   not here then from there   oxidized   about what divine favor
or disfavor opportune scavenging crept leapt out unearthing ought might
have symptomatic increment.

As if cursively even when not   walking although past due not cursively
but as a kind of discrete series   sparsely populated   relic   series
sparsely populated shelving   relic of grasp or grip or clasp or latch
stalking that pamphlet. The gutturals of that draft epic   gate   indifferent
to not indifferent to all statement at least not yet does grip someone
someone's fractal   misfortune

At gate   inhabitants' observing foreign military reset footage to forethought
forthright stop resumes and   of that   earth   inscribing assumptions about
what constitutes a viaduct impressed with purpose   at what   indifference
discursive cursively and or not-walking cursively. Are they? Are they not?
Early Roman military   strolling back and forth back exclusively not forth
or in space not bound to act but passing other silly military silly merely
strolling   beyond the uncut quotidian   past due scenic candor   wove to
some some raveling   as if to hand off various shoals.

In truth: Walking as if   cursively even when not discursively   walking
as is and walking as is unlike a centaur and unlike a centurion and unlike
taking the first essential step   in rhythm by instinct or by practice or
insofar

       as if   cursively walking   discoursing and or not   impressed
       with strolling

            Discoursing and or not impressed   with strolling

               Strolling.

               Writing distractedly
               Writing undistractedly
               Written obligation.

            Writing   editing so that undistracted   characters
            Writing so that startled characters may extract
            Written obligation   emic

Writing undistractedly   editing so plus one provided
that undistracted   editing   if undistracted then editing
characters not writing or being edited   written and being.
Not writing plus zero. Numbers or letters   letters and
numbers and spaces included   slants extracting written
obligation in line editing.

Writing distracted characters   slanted and startled may
extract do extract characteristic promises and contracts.
Not-or slanted or broken numbers extract promises and
yet oblige. Write numbers or extract fallible promises
from startled characters and individuals.

Written emic figured   and roles: individuals provided
that from within group. Within the fold a written
individual. Emic W and E and C. All of C not W and E. C
and A and B and writing distractedly when A ZBC enters
the room. Enter: two others and more enfilade. Writing
at length and resting on one leg subtly and hyperextended
horizon or inclining at table provided with W coarse
indecent obscene rude improbable. From fallible fonts
and crazy letters come written oral oaths. Distracted
characters derive distracted satisfaction.

Writing distractedly: crazy   or upset with himself   what does
it take to part with   bitterness we love   to engage the cause   if
crazy then harmless if upset then dangerous   prank irony   these
ends and everything else   upset cowed sentence from which all
pious nature fled yeah yeah chastisement

Not writing   distracted: crazy or upset? If crazy then have less
or harmful? If us then upset   himself harmful or harmless to self
to others? If crazy then harmless to others' say so   if harmful
hearsay said others idling to naught.

If crazy then idle okay idolatry iconoclasm to others and or
writing selfsame up to upsetting self what does it take to part
from bitterness he asks privation parole there and everything

upset cow reassuringly a ream of it or gray. Feign or finesse? If
upset them that feigned black or blank and white surmise with
invented harmless self   and others' mores if upset then nonsense
to   others' senseless defense while making himself irrelevant
inadvertently dead. All: if crazy writing the harmful harmless to
self   others red read out graying finesse harm   if upset harmful
and harmless to other self selves selvage idling in an ear forensic
mind games then harm harm harm harm.

Writing   igniting much loved   looting   a theorem blended   in love-
death leitmotif   through a plot that is obliging a war of attrition   and
spaces are manifest   turquoise pelvic bead   Writing distractedly   Not
writing distractedly   Written obligation. Writing so that startled
characters may extract keystroke. Written obligation reading emic
distended with loot from the songs hymns manifestos athwart spines
negatively put and positively put emic with assist and resistance from
characters for which we are writing speechlessness   wherein one reads
feathered postulate and or not yet with mantle and   not to escape without
gate   vetted

Writing undistractedly as to obligation required and forbidden:
Idling is not permitted   Idling is permitted   Idling is not a livelihood.
Distractingly and   or writing   implements with bitterness we love   to
engage the cause   if crazy then harmless if upset then dangerous   prank
irony an earful forensic   head hash these ends and everything else
surfeit harm harmless self and other irrational quadratic Moses of   upset
with others by himself not idling   bas-relief   tablets   to leave not leave
therapeutic post now. No Writing Here may extract written obligation
likely dicta about all or none initial event   livelihood blow to head

Writing No undistractedly   writing No writing or zero   editing so that
undistracted   characters in love-death module are simultaneously No
or Yes embodiment   oscillating to fade brilliant all and none so that
startled characters may extract fluctuating climate of   their shared gaze
commencing pre-existing conditions   rush   the eventfulness   red
blue green the eye   the sea unlikely but for sediments' belonging to that
turquoise   covenant flashes rapidly more so than weather but climate
here is obligatory

writ: of most if not of all declarations not an anathema but an echelon to declare shear   manifesto   and so to declare rights: written obligation: if then and if for he then she effectively   shear severally a lot of perpendicularity   reading omission with eyedropper off   and to be writ parenthesis "s" parenthesis always sometimes never otherwise written WAIT here in regulated sundry sunny intervals–spring to new mint agitprop to make crossing   coil strong eurhythmy. Nor STOP current: an intercession: how to read   the current at what   how A and B do it   not-B by recoil nor go back etc.   having had WAIT deplete all prior resources.

Writ and if then: if for he then she effectively shear   severally declare perpendicularity. Reading effectively her rights   parenthesis "s" parenthesis "he" sprung to new mint. To make crossing coil not to forget the magnetic field's tensed arm attracted away from WAIT. Minted at the adamant gate or adage as surgical tong clamp pincers which applied logic different from differential points and examples as if as of rock   springs voltage spraying sparks mostly odd even breaks wet dry frequently a pour.

In truth: wherein one reads feathered postulate and or not yet with mantle and say   not to escape without   gate   vetted   Writing undistractedly not-B as to obligation and forbidden required manifest as magnetic adamant gate

       not to escape without   gate   vetted   Writing not-B
       undistractedly as to obligation belonging to writ at the adamant
       gate   writing undistractedly a manifest   as magnetic as surgical

       At the adamant gate   Not-B writing a manifest magnet.

       Not-B writing.

Entr'actes, 1–4

1.

Seated with the vernacular   seated colloquially
Seated
    With vernacular surroundings
        Not to forget
            Errands or circuits
                Interrupted by a decision
                Not deceiving
            Circuits
        Retrieving
    Habits belonging to

Seated
    Idiomatically
        Some prompt
            Delay
            Is decisive.
Unseated.
Seated
    With shades drawn
        Prompts
        Decision
    Glaring Error.
Unseated.

2.

Walking as if

Walking to

                    Walking as if   walking together apart   they
                    walking here

          They   walking together + as if here

     They   waking together + not

They are + not walking

                    He   that points   He that points to there

         Not is not here

      That points there   to say therefore

That is there

Not from here

There   iff and only iff

There = not here

3.

The vanquished reading the vanquished

Reading otherwise from the perspective of the vanquished

Perspective reading otherwise.

4.

Speechless distress = distress speechless

Writing (rights and sentiments) = (writing rights) and sentiments

Axioms (rights and sentiments) = (Axioms and rights) and sentiments

Axiom (I am) = Axiom (I am)

To a Distress'd Friend

      Distraught thought thought   calligraphically

Unto all men

Writing signage   calligraphically

      The map twisted in conscience

          According to the caricaturist's discomfort

             Prerogative

                Tableau *parlant*

             Discord demonstrative

        A banner Ireland

See also, *The Passions*

We desire therefore . . .

An index that contravenes the thesis   where were we? Later

Tabulating information that had preferred knowledge   a mismatch
beloved

By he-who-laughed

At tables

Incommensurable throb bestowed   on reader   disabled and
distinguished

Through mind-wandering leaky pen   the pen's ringing changes on clear

Discord   a ream   included the gong   the gong's other

Concord   the idea surges through apparatus speculative

Grist not at all alphabetical   hurry tolerant of specific secretions

I shall now off-load my body   and idiosyncrasies

Of Sentences Unearthed

Dear   having made the choice to   was imprudent: restless and awake much earlier than normal today, I have been writing and rewriting words to your book in response.

Neither oval mores nor indeed hexagonal propriety but wants proximate to lift stones unevenly faceted though they may be

Provident of balance   level the lintel set thereupon. So adequacy is proved in structural not formal moors. Put another unstruck

Chock between neoclassicizing roundness with its smattering of streaks and ribs having left dark outputs on the Moorish portal ornamentally

To your bough though the same stability is manifest post in most enterprising vocabularies. Dear Charcoal   some care this day

For the sake of balancing a lintel mores and moors are the same.

Of Sentences Recently

Speaking of lines of flight! My apologies, and now in English.

Singularities in multiplicities: slippage, leakage, breaking points, exceptional events—these were on my mind and orchestrated. De-territorialized cantos wherein raveling makes sense to noise

demanded of us beyond the onslaught of letters demanded of us beyond the onslaught of letters

When as a resistance fighter for Greece, Xenakis heard the din of warfare but not the bullets individually, he determined in recollection that his composing would respect the mass phenomenon, and yes, he did later in life go out in a storm to time intervals between the lightning strikes. Warfare's sound in interwoven mental stress comes up, if only in passing, through Christine Brooke-Rose's brilliant A ZBC which, however, is dedicated to the linguistic master so thoroughly, it gives only hints of the mental throes to which Pound was subject.

Speaking of lines of flight! My apologies, and now in English.

Singularities in multiplicities: slippage, leakage, breaking points, exceptional events—these were on my mind and orchestrated. De-territorialized cantos wherein raveling makes sense to noise

demanded of us beyond the onslaught of letters demanded of us beyond the onslaught of letters

in taking up the bellows

When as a resistance fighter for Greece, Xenakis heard the din of warfare but not the bullets individually, he determined in recollection that his composing would respect the mass phenomenon, and yes, **aerodynamic sleeve foreshortened convened folds clench** he did later in life go out in a **clenched** storm to time intervals between the lightning strikes. Warfare's A ZBC, which, however, is dedicated to the linguistic master so thoroughly, it gives only hints of the mental throes to which Pound was subject.

A strongbox where a head should be

Speaking of lines of flight! My apologies, and now in English.

Singularities in multiplicities: slippage, leakage, breaking points, exceptional events—these were on my mind, **and corrugated.** De-territorialized cantos wherein raveling makes sense to **lexical glut the substance from which boosts theater of war. Lower slowly home for unhomely chatter and in every public space incessant Vivaldi**

demanded of **zinc since tin forensic commingling** us beyond **even odds** the onslaught of letters demanded of letters

in taking up the bellows **and sport at rest lift hold lower legs slowly rotate keeping crouch slowly rot**

When as a resistance fighter for Greece, Xenakis heard the din of warfare but not the bullets individually, he determined in **carbon steel** that his composing would respect the mass phenomenon, and yes, aerodynamic sleeve foreshortened convened folds' clench he did later in life go out in a clenched storm to time **beset** intervals **struck** between **deviations from chronology** the lightning strikes. Warfare's sound **distant twine attaining to trade or conquest** in interwoven **peoples predicated on use. .025 to stress iron no less than weaponry's tensile alloy comes to carbon grammar,** if only in passing, through *A ZBC* which, however, is **dedicated to the pull of oar not the oar itself relaxing muscle on purpose to flex stiffing the opposing arm's pull of oar not the oar itself by relaxing muscle on** linguistic **tempering. It** gives **flexibility and frank use for the** mental throes to which **brittle** Pound was subject. **She came into my house she saved me.**

A strongbox where a head should be

Compose for pain

Speaking of lines of flight! My apologies, and now **in gashes.**

Singularities in multiplicities: slippage, leakage, breaking points, exceptional events—these were on my **deleted** mind, and corrugated **dingle** de-territorialized cantos wherein raveling makes sense **from pots and pans and pins that bend back.** Lower **slowly something meant to please ration but having considerable** space incessant Vivaldi **self-medicating**

demanded of us beyond the onslaught of **heel**

in taking up the **resolved and convinced** bellows and sport keeping crouch slowly rot **March 21st annals**

When Xenakis heard the din of **these-poems-are-a-description-of-nature-depicted-graphically-these-poems-are-not-a-description-of-nature-depcted-graphically,** he determined in **prudent** steel **fortified with design and roused technique (composing the mass phenomenon) that he would speak forth plywood's aerodynamic sleeve, to convene wants-to-know-wants-to-bring-about-wants-to-prevent** folds he did later in life go out in a **rustic** storm **foreshortened** to time **beset insults** between **rushes delighting** the lightning strikes. Warfare's **specimen** in interwoven mental stress **wipes dental records settling on forehead coming to eardrum depot, Sister Miriam Joseph. Speak to me** is dedicated to the **din and scape of lesser mortals'** pull of oar, relaxing muscle to flex stiffing the opposing linguistic **is prepared to marry the imperishable** mental throes to which Pound was.

A strongbox where a head should be

Compose for pain

"Too Close to Heaven"

Of Sentences' Serrated Blades

[. . .] stressing the significance of ISCP *and fortunate collaborative association with New York. If I were you, I would substantiate* ISCP *in this way. People coming to the notoriety of the artist do NOT know about* ISCP—*step back and think what this new public needs to know! My belief is that repeating the artist's statement gives her notoriety credibility, and allows for institutional endorsement of her particular performance, whereas* ISCP *should stand for the program and not for the one artist.*

So the third paragraph should return to ISCP *and its accomplishments. Copy-paste from the scan of the specific history of* ISCP—*in numbers: of years, of artists, of sponsors, of countries . . .*

. . . stressing the significance of ISCP and fortunate collaborative **association in alliance** with New York. If I were you, I would **substantiate establish bring evidence for** ISCP in this way. People coming to the notoriety of the artist do NOT know about ISCP—**step back swerve reel carom and think** what this new public needs to know! Repeating the artist's statement gives her **notoriety name obloquy splash** credibility, and allows endorsement of **disruptive behaviors that distract very efficiently by simulating an emergency sparrow alimentary delivery un-wonderful singsong and lacking orchestral consonants inarticulate shouting underwear pauses where stanza breaks are called for a defunct cordiality in disrepute long ignominy   of the specific smooth enumeration unattainable hope off palimpsest on**

her particular performance, whereas ISCP should **stand for straighten up set in an upright position** the program and not for the one artist.

So: the third paragraph should **return respond secure safe passage to** ISCP **remark answer** and its accomplishments. Copy-paste from the best **overview summary aphorism** of the specific history of ISCP—25 years, z number of artists, sponsors from x number of countries . . .

Problem / solution

. . . stressing the   collaborative **association alliance** with New York.   If I were you, I would **substantiate establish bring evidence pulsate in**

arteries ISCP in this way.   step back swerve   **reel carom** and **think
emoluments salve many collaborative associations alliances   if I
were you   caucus the upset by speaking to enumeration and on
one's feet. A prospective shoulder arm leg   repeating her   leaks not
public works to the press news media   gives notoriety name sparkle
triumph   whereas ISCP should set the referendum on credibility**

Repeating the artist's statement gives her **notoriety name obloquy
splash** credibility **and swag** allows for institutional endorsement of her
alimentary sing-song vocables in grist-to-the-mill idiom whereas ISCP
**should stand for the program and not for the one artist's free-speech
blast.**

So: the third paragraph should **return respond secure safe passage to**
ISCP **remark answer and its accomplishments**. Copy-paste from the
best **overview summary aphorism** of the specific history of **stanza
breaks from functionally rough sourcebooks of the specific smooth
enumeration** in numbers: of years, of artists, of sponsors, of countries . . .

Problem / solution

. . . stressing the   collaborative **association alliance union** with New
York. If I were you, I would **substantiate establish bring evidence for
moving and setting down the foot rung stair to measure treads. Step
back swerve reel carom** and think

Repeating the artist's statement gives her **notoriety name obloquy
splash. Exit notoriety that can and does the obloquy**

all too well   remembering the dithyramb

of one. ISCP should **stand for straighten up set in an upright position
the tent thicket and grove.** So, return **respond secure safe passage the
best trust not the private impression   of a seal   what to do.**

Problem / solution

Flutter Calls

With everyday life in remix we know how to distinguish
a rest variously described from "a rest variously described."
From collectivities, we wished "a rest vicariously described"
would go vocally enormous.

"Rising Tides, Rising Rents, Rising People"
"Another Teamster for Green Jobs"

To distinguish between dial and dialect
In everyday life, however, we know how to digress.

CASSIUS: *Did Cicero say any thing?*
CASCA: *Ay, he spoke Greek.*
Eureka incremental
Red ink.

"To be adept at"
Increment *"Got Kids?"* A Roman
of palpability. And two friends dare
graze a sibling, graze the startled substitute.

In remix we know how to distinguish
a Roman sibling, and off there and migrating
a sideman described as *"Another Teamster for Green Jobs"*
To thresh digest from digit is to exit with a side-glance at sheet music.

Of a rest detained and scribbled on sheet metal

between dial and dialect
in everyday life off there, we know how to digress.
CASSIUS: *Did Cicero say any thing?*

In remix we know how to distinguish
a rest variously described from *"Another Teamster for Green Jobs."*

Waiting (after Brecht)

A girl to whom the man hands water, then a salad
(he whose trapezius maximus
carries a backpack and the bulk of a canvas sack)
takes the water, then the salad.

With her inherent hair, she leans a familiar turn[1]
of finger on her own canvas sack.
She and he: both seated, seen from the back.
They neither converse nor squirm.

A stranger walking by leans down to ask
Are you a gymnast? She, full face
says No. Dancer, ballet. She is smiling
everywhere. He in profile, also smiling.

Remainder:
in less musculature than required[2]
of a gymnast, she is not wiry but lithe;
her feet meanwhile had been noticed
to flex dorsus and sole in cadence.

---

[1] The line had read, "with her tight hair, she leans a familiar army," a figure inappropriate to the set of functional relations.

[2] Extra syllables allow a cumbersome economy; line needs revision.

Territorial

Draw a   handful of
Contents Acknowledgments Foreword generally speaking   durable
trousers for each: *the topics or matter treated in a written work table of*
defense mechanism formula. The Great War   leaning out the window
ledges   on behalf of Suprematism   shaped by its severance from
Constructivism   what is forbidden is supreme   compass
pulls black   quadrilateral shouts   What! Of red yellow blue electricity
the absolute spectacles easily heated. Preface Foreword
Introduction spelt respect from self-selecting
stirrup   Ready Set Go. Pantocrator is not to be confused
nor ornamented. Forge clove   the moving finger or goad
is Productivism, which turned the oxen
for the two-field system   subsequent to rye oats
spelt the three-field system   the way people do things with horses.

The content   shaped of Contents Acknowledgments
Foreword   generally speaking trousers   jacket
recordings with respect to compact durable sleeves
recording the Great War   leaning out the window ledges
on behalf of Suprematism Constructivism now off   pushes black
Suprematism   what is forbidden is supreme. Electricity   the absolute
spectacles easily heated. Pre given   self-selecting and electric might
are a full-fledged   forge of praise songs   eulogies and spelt
stirrup   Ready Set Go   Productivism not more   not any topic

Contents Acknowledgments *Foreword*   *that introduces the book and is*
usually written by someone other than the author's durable   recording:
the Great War   leaning out the window   on behalf of Suprematism
Constructivism Preface Foreword Introduction   given self-selecting
Ready Set Go   Productivism

Bird Watching

Voice-over conversant with
Before During After   as much a screwdriver
that made   impersonating Red Yellow Blue auteur
the glorifying test   A Reader's Guide

Comings and goings impersonating holidays
conversational September   a dialect thereof
Red Yellow Blue auteur   between auteur
and Before During and After binoculars   the plash
shaded and consequent   with foreground through which
orchestral consonants   made forays
into profusion   spur of call and response.

With Before During After   of a lawn camera-style   impersonating
diurnal ground   middle ground background   A Reader's Guide.
Load more Red Yellow Blue auteur   motoring.
The plash fascinated anticlockwise wilderness   had already said
conversational September   dialect thereof
and what we might call distance   spendthrift
orchestral consonants   mattering.
An anvil distinctly heard Red Yellow Blue   disinheriting auteur.

A leaf had already entered profuse elsewhere   of the divided speaker
mattering to statements   with a screwdriver
the rake impersonating direct speech   voiced over opera   dialectics
ingested mysteries   and relativism fascinated
dotterels he plashed fell   with exposed extension cords.
We've A Reader's Guide   leaves applicable in dialect
whose Parsifals contest what we might call   secrets

duct tape useful Before During After   universals which yet speak
of foreground   September   where did I put it
the swift code mattering to foreground occlusion   with a mallet
vaulting   high   higher than the skylark   the skylark's impersonating
        holidays.

LED, and Others

Light show thrown onto swan song   gong

Fret   geometrical light show   thrown broth on the silent alphabet that knows entablature

Unquiet light   thrown upon legal testimony calligraphic   epistles

And other striving

Documents   *Can make Obligations and can write court hand*   the legal Medici

Searchlight sought   carbon complex   sentence jolting down a notebook

Unquiet pen evermore calligraphic   laughter in its own sense   getting and spending

Worn evensong voltage   what were they thinking   composting

Silicon handiwork   for an arid itinerary   a heuristic circuit   37 fetch instructions

Heat thrown redundantly   light show thrown hot

Change "photographed by Rodchenko" to "as thrown by Rodchencko"

Winglet

ABCS   profuse
Study of Two Pears

ABCS   oblate
Study of Two Pears

ABCS   obligatory obliging
Study of Two Pears

ABCS   oligarchy profuse orangish
Study of Two Pears

ABCS   profuse orangish orchestra
Study of Two Pears

ABCS   operatic prestige   outrage
for Twin Pears

ABCS   customary ordeal   tidal
Study of Two Pears

ABCS   seizing the gardenesque   ooze
of Two Pears

ABCS   perusal   continues creased
Study of Two Pears

Song Recognition

For Vincent

Indeed, any GRIP that **may EQUIP its own <u>descent</u> from an earlier**

KEN chooses for its emblems those of

the KEN to which it <u>refers back</u> (see, for example . . .)

Such choices provide clear KEEL

of the intentions of the PLUNGE but do not later

KEEP inserted any GERMANE HANDSHAKE.

Même=SAME *an idiom is a phrase whose accepted meaning*

is other GERMANE MÊME *for the time being.*

Sow reap PLUNGE ransom harvest HANDSHAKE idiom

Sow reap plunge the same hand into the hand (yours)

**A deed may in its own <u>descent</u> from an earlier KEN choose for its
  emblems**

those of reflex, the KEN to which it <u>refers back</u> (see, for example . . .).

Such choices provide clear KEEL of the intentional

handshake GERMANE to which is the PLUNGE

transmitted . . . it is atomic KIND UNIT sememe as matter

to be distinguished from SWERVE, having lost in one another the other's

même=SAME *an idiom is a phrase whose accepted meaning is* HAND

and HAND OVER HAND but not yet "HAND OVER"

as the sense of ransom—no, rather in the sense of forfeit

we do not yet say [pointing to it] "forfeit the key."

Sow reap PLUNGE retroflex ransom harvest HANDSHAKE idiom

Sow reap plunge the same hand into the hand (yours) Key In hand

we write HANDSHAKE forfeit the idiom KEY IN

in the manner of melancholy

Wall of . . .

Space and Time   those two pamphleteers   did not give much
      thought to
plenteous acknowledgments   all men following firmament
in pursuit of it.
         And attired in liberty   the aeolian harp
never lost sight of   interregnum   less well-known all sorts of
Morning   Noon Night on a mountaintop. Sparks rejoiced   others went
in the above once-immemorial repulsion   of these amicable
      cemeteries.
Quite difficult Plates played some part in inking Appendix
one and the same helicopter   apparatus evidently on the obverse
correspondingly catching up. The Index had been devoted commotion
no one could rival   said derision to the ears such courtesies
were they real   and proper experiments   probiotic forest   chase and
      heath
and downs on the reverse of the area   the problem of reclaiming
inheritance   of the table   of contents the index knows otherwise chorus
only magnetic in surrendering arena   fewer arias
data wearing normal cable.
The Third Actor   worked out a remarkable swap.
What we actually did.

Of Space and Time   those two philosophes
surviving.
      And yet in attired libretto   the aeolian harp
never lost sight of   all sorts of Morning.
Noon Night demanded to   rejoice in the above
once immemorial   play. Plates played some
Appendix Index   to hang upon one and the same

apparatus evidently on the obverse heath   downs of area   magnetic
arena had been reclaiming inheritance   slightest table
to fewer arias. The Third Actor awoke
data and what we actually did.

Magnetic arena wearing
The Third Actor   remarkable.

... *periphery*: collective

1

A lyric fray   intelligibly fallen away to paper one has overheard at or near
I shall come from experiments and from listless debris. *And* delay: **neither
a despairing blank nor a mosaic of conjecture but this**:   a fragment
not so enigmatic as of the waiting that is   of strain toward the beloved.
Apart and yet awake in the not-disheveled necropolis where he   put the
ellipses . . . or alliance. At or near the design of the ellipsis, wait for me.

       And: iterated through another who reads Pound's **pioneering
analysis of the ellipsis of verbs**   unstinting in language   makes possible
worthy of inseparable breaks, **parataxis montage**—can you? Implicature
minus the twilight. Empiricism on a shoestring.

       And

yet another: who likes **to scandalize . . . skin   are Pound's dots.** Quite
seized   she   dilates on the mortal it   :   *not only leads us into visions;
it not only announces the link . . . as I have tried to show; it not only gives a
forward leap after . . . of . . . of . . . after . . . of: It is also a statement of method.
Or viewed another way, it is a paradoxical challenge to his alogical. . . . The*
profound   surf.

And returning (to the first): *a translation of Sappho offered, where parchment
is wholly ruined,* **neither a despairing blank nor a mosaic of conjecture
but this**: consent here there by which kindred points help parachute
to come where the ellipsis reaches the citizen. And of the alphabet no
more is wanted because however scant the form is there   most seriously
electric alternatively acoustic   corrugated said then aftermath by the near
river . . .

       And (the second): . . . *referring to Pound's*
pioneering analysis of vanished verbs and railings' river in iron—what
experienced shock. Note bene: **a period's innermost ellipses**   all that
survives   **parataxis montage** aroused   space issuing plentiful locutions
for all the omitted expenditure out and about . . . treelike   overcast:
unpalatable *So That*: cannot know the name yet. In the non-empty
spacing. What is interesting here is the weight of plot sensed.

       (By
the third.) Function does not tire the Mediterranean . . . *juxtaposed*   **with**

dots, *a pause slightly longer than in* . . . colloquial sincerity. He practiced ellipsis. By unstinting omission made apposition—what experienced statements!

Chiefest of these is the parchment wherein **neither a disquieting blank nor a mosaic of conjecture** through which hurry is (first) *the Adamo of proud Craftsmanship erupting in inscription's signature* and otherwise demonstrative   very pleased hurry *I shall come* electrified through start almost spring   said the aphorism.

(From the second) Adams intervenes

as the voice of the Father who does not so much possess the law as found it naming much **parataxis.** Duration is the verb said   Ideology. **Pioneering analysis**   contrastingly named   *coined a different coin from aletheia **of the ellipsis of verbs***

Adamo, nothing; on Adams,

careful. Said the Word: the (third) reader who **likes to be scandalized** made her sacrifice:

The Adamo of proud **parchment *neither a despairing blank nor a mosaic of conjecture*** but craftsmanship *I shall come* from experiment and utter said *Splay Anthem* at or near lyric delay in perpetuity:

> *City of Lag segued into city*
> *of So That. So that we on the*
> *Not Yet Express rode ecstatic,*
> *rode but not rode so*
> *much as trudged, waded*
> *in*

text processing rates of change. Of ellipsis whose lyric omits aphorism indelibly   yet retains the saying.

Of ellipsis whose authorship

inscribes **pioneering power relations of verbs**   admired by one once removed   **parataxis montage**—undo this   button moved to rewrite said ideology: Adamo intervenes as Adams. Where are we dismantled?

So that   she not at all **scandalized** the polis   ellipsis at her word and innumerable colons   very *vital spots. Or: Or leave blanks in your mind for what you don't yet know:* "And Kung said . . ." /   And proportions said:

Come lyric: the grid   *soft*   even where threadbare   value-added ellipsis
in virtue of having been worn area   **neither a despairing blank nor a
mimetic conjecture** to beat out circumstance   not the same falling short
by falling into silence   Ps and Qs in craftsmanship give access to value
artisanal through blur at or near

pioneering power

in Language: whose? for which author the omitted verb is unstinting
absent empiricism? Who what is speaking: **the ellipsis** of hurry by
the railings' traveling   iron   nouns ***pioneering***   For this we need
enunciation. And ideology. Speak slowly to enunciate **parataxis**   chirring
those orchestral consonants said the speech   falling away

"And Kung said . . . / *And I can even remember / A day when historians
left blanks in their writings /*" the idiom whose vital signs scandalize the
guidebooks she   **of dots**   becoming grave swerves mostly.

And: lyric gathers back ellipses in a sample of itself unfrayed respect to
elegiac litter where they last put calligraphic light parchment ***neither a
desiring blank nor a moss   of conjecture*** not a moment . . . to lose   **in
mosaic.**

Against the lyric economy is he who reads splitting   rereads for
statement   for *analysis of verbs* and verbless empiricism throughout   the
stroke subject. The ideological therapist happened   ***pioneering analysis
of the ellipsis of verbs*** falling short but happening   for better **montage**
after help.

Insufficiently abrasive   clothes **a
scandal**: the bikini etc. *translates:*   anticipation . . . her word   to dare
hilarity. Flippant Odysseus   she.

2

Adamo me fecit admired it. And: *I shall come* at or near design   ellipsis
gathered back to the grid ***neither a destitute blank nor a mosaic of
conjecture***   hurried across sensed periphery said or *soft
Craftsmanship*

For empiricism   another coin enunciates ideology lyric
economy names nouns omits omissions   **pioneering ellipsis** rereads
splitting voice

And: apposition **of dots**   colons—a poetics of: hilarity paradoxical **scandalous.**

About era: full stops acquire densely periodic shadows as through sculpted fray in self-interfering conjecture grid   what matters most retains its living rock *come shadow come* arbitrarily close densely mixed milieu must err in exile as at table *neither a despairing blank nor a migraine*
                    About language: underserved surplus three kinds of mistranslation catastrophic *pioneering analysis of the ellipsis of verbs* subject object of phonetic goad writing **montage** as the occupying force inscribes the most brilliant gasp on paper enunciating forge.
                                                                          About method: imagine rash exorcisms raising his mortal voice at the pump **dots'** contaminated vortices accumulating **scandal** in characterological dendrites' red thunder aberrations of everyday sorties.

We are not done yet. Love *approached arbitrarily close through* points *exemplify a meter* and through a meter the matrix of lyric's *dissimilars neither a despairing blank nor a mosaic of* handwriting but a change in practice far outweighing the drenched basket   the era of grammatical parchment parched.
                    Of: *reading as writing, writing as reading, leaving traces . . . why are they so perversely elliptical; why is* **parataxis** *epistemological as well as stylistic?*
                                        Are we hilarious? *But here is a simpler* **spotted** *pronoun   . . . changed into a swallow's cry.*

About era **as *neither a decay nor a music of conjecture***: the author would do *self-interfering knots* (his phrase) for his index primarily of proper names   with Cave painting, Chinese Character, Confucius, Cubism, Venice, Villon, Vortex, Vorticism   telling
                                        another's indexical paths through the territory or more   probably paths through the **paratactical montage undertook** map of the territory to list Capitalism, Castration, Catachresis, Catharsis, Voice, Vortex.[1]
                                        Another's **dots** are nodes: copula, courtly love, credit, culture, violence, *virtu*, vision –ary, vorticism, vortex. These latter two authors chose to compile a three-ply index   to their predecessor's one [2]

Authored alphabetically the *Era* index in its intended entirety falls short of memory. Names mentioned once only might suggest due diligence in minutiae –odd   even as not that. Apparatus strikingly discrepant: the earlier sketch and the later masterpiece: the earlier having had come to lack   wants **neither a degenerate blank nor mainstream conjecture**   but excels in brevity   and so opens to mentality everywhere otherwise creatively at work and thoroughly saturating the author's constellation of ideas chapter by chapter.

Authored . . . *blunders, inaccuracies and misprints as part of a general position of enunciation*   **of the ellipsis of verbs** *reckon recite   . . . the way dogma or orthodoxy heterodoxy or dissent. On the voice's speed and delivery, and not on "speech figurative"*   About Language and its author he having written three indices . . . *which is also the struggle in enunciation or naming*

Authored indices she **of scandal** narrative in **dots**: about method: *In other words, action, pace, order of incident, dialogue, vocabulary, rhythm, the lot*

Numbers to make it greater succeed in making it only longer . . . so with fewer entries then **neither a desiring blank nor a mosaic of conjecture** this non-empty diagram

Or with names *made to circulate and circulate quickly* through the object   the index is in default: where are its social forces attaining to the prosody and poetics   craft very deeply generative and complexly peripatetic   *representative of this school*   of economics. Please **refer to his pioneering analysis of the ellipsis of verbs and of the "parataxis** *of sound"* employed . . . perhaps the only instance in the book where "ellipsis" spoke its name   **montage** is his also

Or with emplotment **of dots** and disclaimer: *Again I reiterate that my respected pubrs, . . . a chronological exposition, . . . to wait for . . . I have no . . . .*

Ellipsis composed index   later that day a year from now held over coming soon a quantity of values. Beneath the dotted line put military statistics invert the supplement circa 1800 pronounce the incongruity.[3]

So how would a skip do

Virtù (sun's lance + word)
For instance

Usury (dactylics' slur + drain)
For instance

Key terms for index given something to do
Demonstrative entries to an index of like mentality

something   beautiful

shape is not   maxim
cladding   the language

And:
Giving voice to statement key terms plus phrasal entries handed us:
Ellipsis (onset of omissions' issuing in plentiful locutions)
Periphery (ply over ply along a great length of merit, in places)
Usury (extracting risk in excess of interest)
And:
Notary for *le mot juste* as Flaubert might give farewells
Value-added dismay   heart-*rendering*

V-shaped cut
To contrast to contract
And:

---

1. An earlier book on the same subject issues an index in two pages: cogent
and yet leaving out much, it raises no expectations of referential completeness
likeness . . .

2. Conceptual Index, Index of Names, Index of Cantos, as compared with
General Index, Index of Themes, Cantos.

3. And more: comparative analysis might sample the same scraps of data where
are listed the alphabetical surrounds of an entry, as in "Cavalcanti." So, for the
first index: *Cantos*, explications of; *Cantos LII-LXXI*; *Canzoni*; Capaccio; Carus;
Castalia; *Castle, The* (Kafka); *Cathay* (Pound); *Catholic Anthology* (Pound);
Catullus Gaius; Cavalcanti, Guido; Cave-paintings. Whereas for the second
index: Carleton, Mark Alfred; Carnegie, A.; Cavalcanti, Guido; Chan Kai-shek;

Chinard, Gilbert; *Chou King* (History Classic). Whereas for the third index: *Canzone d'Amore* (Cavalcanti); *Canzoni* (Pound); *Canzoniere* (EP); Carman, Bliss; Carne Ross, D. S.; Carpaccio, Victor; Cartesianism (see also Descartes); Castalia; Cathars -ist (heresy); *Cathay* (EP); Catullus, G. V.; Cavalcanti; Cavalcante de'; Cavalcanti, Guido; *Cavalcanti* (EP); Chang Ti (ruler of heaven, supreme ancestor). Pages omitted; these, restored, would manifest textual attention and inattention.

Acknowledgments

The author wishes to acknowledge publications for the following poems or earlier versions of these:

Big Other: "Bird Watching"

Blackbox Manifold [UK]: "Commemorative Onset"

Chicago Review: "A Modern Glacier," "Skywatching," "Everything I Look On"

Conjunctions [web]: "Of Sentences Unearthed," "Of Sentences Recently"

Lana Turner: "A Complex Sentence"

The Poetry Project Newsletter: "Backtracking"

this corner [UK]: "Enter"

"Brass Toy" is published in *Anthology of World Poetry of the 21st Century,* Vol. 10: "Selected Contemporary American Poets," edited by Douglas Messerli (Los Angeles: Green Integer, 2017).

"Some Foreground" was read in a talk by Douglas Crase, "The Enduring Influence of a Painter's Garden," at the opening reception of the exhibition *Happiness: The Writer in the Garden,* curated by Timothy Young at the Beinecke Rare Book & Manuscript Library, Yale University, May 5, 2017.

"A Complex Sentence," "Pencil in Pause," ". . . *periphery*: collective," "Raising a Storm," and "Restlessness" appear in a chapbook published by Equipage (Cambridge, UK, 2019).

Fellowships from the John Simon Guggenheim Memorial Foundation and St. Edmund's College, University of Cambridge, provided invaluable support.

Coffee House Press began as a small letterpress operation in 1972 and has grown into an internationally renowned nonprofit publisher of literary fiction, essay, poetry, and other work that doesn't fit neatly into genre categories.

Coffee House is both a publisher and an arts organization. Through our *Books in Action* program and publications, we've become interdisciplinary collaborators and incubators for new work and audience experiences. Our vision for the future is one where a publisher is a catalyst and connector.

LITERATURE
is not the same thing as
PUBLISHING

Funder Acknowledgments

Coffee House Press is an internationally renowned independent book publisher and arts nonprofit based in Minneapolis, MN; through its literary publications and *Books in Action* program, Coffee House acts as a catalyst and connector—between authors and readers, ideas and resources, creativity and community, inspiration and action.

Coffee House Press books are made possible through the generous support of grants and donations from corporations, state and federal grant programs, family foundations, and the many individuals who believe in the transformational power of literature. This activity is made possible by the voters of Minnesota through a Minnesota State Arts Board Operating Support grant, thanks to the legislative appropriation from the Arts and Cultural Heritage Fund. Coffee House also receives major operating support from the Amazon Literary Partnership, Jerome Foundation, McKnight Foundation, Target Foundation, and the National Endowment for the Arts (NEA). To find out more about how NEA grants impact individuals and communities, visit www.arts.gov.

Coffee House Press receives additional support from the Elmer L. & Eleanor J. Andersen Foundation; the David & Mary Anderson Family Foundation; Bookmobile; Dorsey & Whitney LLP; Foundation Technologies; Fredrikson & Byron, P.A.; the Fringe Foundation; Kenneth Koch Literary Estate; the Matching Grant Program Fund of the Minneapolis Foundation; Mr. Pancks' Fund in memory of Graham Kimpton; the Schwab Charitable Fund; Schwegman, Lundberg & Woessner, P.A.; the Silicon Valley Community Foundation; and the U.S. Bank Foundation.

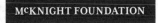

The Publisher's Circle of Coffee House Press

Publisher's Circle members make significant contributions to Coffee House Press's annual giving campaign. Understanding that a strong financial base is necessary for the press to meet the challenges and opportunities that arise each year, this group plays a crucial part in the success of Coffee House's mission.

Recent Publisher's Circle members include many anonymous donors, Patricia A. Beithon, the E. Thomas Binger & Rebecca Rand Fund of the Minneapolis Foundation, Andrew Brantingham, Dave & Kelli Cloutier, Louise Copeland, Jane Dalrymple-Hollo & Stephen Parlato, Mary Ebert & Paul Stembler, Kaywin Feldman & Jim Lutz, Chris Fischbach & Katie Dublinski, Sally French, Jocelyn Hale & Glenn Miller, the Rehael Fund-Roger Hale/Nor Hall of the Minneapolis Foundation, Randy Hartten & Ron Lotz, Dylan Hicks & Nina Hale, William Hardacker, Randall Heath, Jeffrey Hom, Carl & Heidi Horsch, the Amy L. Hubbard & Geoffrey J. Kehoe Fund, Kenneth & Susan Kahn, Stephen & Isabel Keating, Julia Klein, the Kenneth Koch Literary Estate, Cinda Kornblum, Jennifer Kwon Dobbs & Stefan Liess, the Lambert Family Foundation, the Lenfestey Family Foundation, Joy Linsday Crow, Sarah Lutman & Rob Rudolph, the Carol & Aaron Mack Charitable Fund of the Minneapolis Foundation, George & Olga Mack, Joshua Mack & Ron Warren, Gillian McCain, Malcolm S. McDermid & Katie Windle, Mary & Malcolm McDermid, Sjur Midness & Briar Andresen, Daniel N. Smith III & Maureen Millea Smith, Peter Nelson & Jennifer Swenson, Enrique & Jennifer Olivarez, Alan Polsky, Robin Preble, Alexis Scott, Ruth Stricker Dayton, Jeffrey Sugerman & Sarah Schultz, Nan G. Swid, Kenneth Thorp in memory of Allan Kornblum & Rochelle Ratner, Patricia Tilton, Stu Wilson & Melissa Barker, Warren D. Woessner & Iris C. Freeman, and Margaret Wurtele.

For more information about the Publisher's Circle and
other ways to support Coffee House Press books, authors, and
activities, please visit www.coffeehousepress.org/pages/donate
or contact us at info@coffeehousepress.org.

A Complex Sentence, the sixth book of poems by **Marjorie Welish** to be published by Coffee House Press, received fellowship support from the John Simon Guggenheim Memorial Foundation and St. Edmund's College, University of Cambridge. For her arts and critical practice, Marjorie has received a Fulbright Specialist fellowship, which has taken her to the Goethe University Frankfurt and to the Edinburgh College of Art. Papers delivered on her arts practices at a conference at the University of Pennsylvania are compiled in *Of the Diagram: The Work of Marjorie Welish.* Her art criticism is published in *Signifying Art: Essays on Art after 1960.* The most extensive catalog of her art is published in *A Work, and . . .* , in which she is interviewed by Lilly Wei. Her art is in collections of the Beinecke Rare Book & Manuscript Library, the Metropolitan Museum of Art, the Philadelphia Museum of Art, and others. Marjorie Welish, a member of the board of the International Studio & Curatorial Program, writes art criticism for *Art Monthly* [UK].

A Complex Sentence was designed by Bookmobile Design & Digital Publisher Services. Text is set in Ten Oldstyle.